gourmet vegetarian

Published in 2007 by Murdoch Books Pty Limited.
www.murdochbooks.com.au

Murdoch Books Australia
Pier 8/9, 23 Hickson Road
Millers Point NSW 2000
Phone: + 61 (0) 2 8220 2000
Fax: + 61 (0) 2 8220 2558

Murdoch Books UK Limited
Erico House, 6th Floor
93–99 Upper Richmond Road
Putney, London SW15 2TG
Phone: + 44 (0) 20 8785 5995
Fax: + 44 (0) 20 8785 5985

Chief Executive: Juliet Rogers
Publishing Director: Kay Scarlett

Design Manager: Vivien Valk
Concept & Art Direction: Sarah Odgers
Design: Jacqueline Duncan
Editor and Project Manager: Rhiain Hull
Production: Tiffany Johnson and Kita George
Photographer: Jared Fowler
Stylist: Cherise Koch
Food preparation: Alan Wilson
Introduction text: Leanne Kitchen
Recipes developed by the Murdoch Books Test Kitchen

National Library of Australia Cataloguing-in-Publication Data
Gourmet vegetarian. Includes index.
ISBN 978 1 92125 909 8 (pbk.).
1. Vegetarian cookery I. Price, Jane (Jane Paula Wynn).
(Series: Kitchen Classics; 7). 641.5636

A catalogue record for this book is available from the British Library

Printed by 1010 Printing International Limited in 2007. PRINTED IN CHINA.
Reprinted 2007.

CONVERSION GUIDE: You may find cooking times vary depending on the oven you are using. For fan-forced ovens, as a general rule, set the oven temperature to 20°C (35°F) lower than indicated in the recipe. We have used 20 ml (4 teaspoon) tablespoon measures. If you are using a 15 ml (3 teaspoon) tablespoon, for most recipes the difference will not be noticeable. However, for recipes using baking powder, gelatine, bicarbonate of soda (baking soda), small amounts of flour, add an extra teaspoon for each tablespoon specified.

gourmet vegetarian

THE VEGETARIAN RECIPES YOU MUST HAVE

SERIES EDITOR **JANE PRICE**

MURDOCH BOOKS

CONTENTS

A WORLD OF FLAVOURS   6

SNACKS AND STARTERS   8

SALADS AND SIDES   68

PASTA, NOODLES AND RICE   120

CASSEROLES, CURRIES, STIR-FRIES AND BAKES   188

INDEX   250

A WORLD OF FLAVOURS

Every one of the world's great food cultures that is worth its salt has a healthy ratio of vegetarian dishes in its culinary lexicon. Long before tofu burgers and soy-based meat 'substitutes' became vegetarian clichés, Southern Indians were fashioning rice and lentils into idli and dosa, Italians were stuffing cannelloni with spinach and cheese while over in Mexico, ingenious ways with dried beans, avocado, limes, chillies and tortillas had evolved into an edible art form. Since time immemorial, Southeast Asians have been stir-frying tempeh, currying peas and potatoes, and spicing up eggs, snake beans and pumpkin. North African tables are famed for their bedazzling assortment of salads — chickpea and olive and spiced carrot are just a few examples of these. The French also have a super-refined take on meat-free dining. In that country, you might be served grilled vegetables with garlic mayonnaise or platefuls of the classic vegetable 'stew', ratatouille.

Far from being the sub-cultural statement that vegetarianism came to mean in the 60s and 70s, enjoying meatless meals has long been a part of balanced, local diets around the planet. Sometimes, this has been for religious reasons, sometimes out of necessity, but most often, simply because vegetables, pulses and grains are delicious and deserve to be treated as exceedingly worthy ingredients in their own right. By way of an added bonus, all these foods are incredibly good for you too. Between the covers of *Gourmet Vegetarian* you will find a vibrant selection of vegetarian (note that the recipes are vegetarian, not vegan) recipes that make gorgeously fresh, seasonal produce the star of any meal you create. Whether you opt to present pirohki, parsnip gnocchi or potato and zucchini casserole, you'll be amazed by the bold breadth of flavour and the sophistication that vegetarian food has to offer. And who knows what part of the world you'll be taken to in the process?

SNACKS AND STARTERS

BONDAS

2 teaspoons vegetable oil
1 teaspoon brown mustard seeds
1 onion, finely chopped
2 teaspoons grated fresh ginger
4 curry leaves
3 small green chillies, finely chopped
1.25 kg (2 lb 12 oz) all-purpose potatoes, diced and cooked
pinch ground turmeric
2 tablespoons lemon juice
20 g (^{3}/4 oz) chopped coriander (cilantro) leaves
oil, for deep-frying

BATTER
110 g (3^3/4 oz/1 cup) besan (chickpea flour)
30 g (1 oz/^{1}/4 cup) self-raising flour
45 g (1^3/4 oz/^{1}/4 cup) rice flour
^{1}/4 teaspoon ground turmeric
1 teaspoon chilli powder

MAKES 24

Heat a wok over medium heat. Add the oil and swirl to coat the base and side. Add the mustard seeds and stir for 30 seconds, or until fragrant. Add the onion, ginger, curry leaves and chilli and cook for 2 minutes. Add the potato, turmeric and 2 teaspoons water and stir for 2 minutes, or until the mixture is dry. Remove from the heat and cool. Stir in the lemon juice and coriander leaves, then season to taste. Shape into 24 balls, using 1 heaped tablespoon of the mixture for each ball.

To make the batter, sift the flours, turmeric, chilli powder and ^{1}/4 teaspoon salt into a bowl. Make a well in the centre. Gradually whisk in 330 ml (11^1/4 fl oz/1^1/3 cups) water to make a smooth batter.

Fill a wok one-third full of oil and heat to 180°C (350°F), or until a cube of bread dropped into the oil browns in 15 seconds. Dip the balls into the batter, then cook in the hot oil, in batches, for 1–2 minutes, or until golden. Drain on crumpled paper towel and season with salt. Serve hot.

PREPARATION TIME: 30 MINUTES   COOKING TIME: 25 MINUTES

FRIED CHICKPEAS

300 g (10¹/₂ oz) dried chickpeas
oil, for deep-frying
¹/₂ teaspoon mild or hot paprika
¹/₄ teaspoon cayenne pepper

SERVES 6–8

Put the chickpeas in a large bowl, cover with plenty of cold water and soak overnight. Drain well and pat dry with paper towel.

Fill a deep heavy-based saucepan one-third full of oil and heat to 180°C (350°F), or until a cube of bread dropped into the oil browns in 15 seconds. Deep-fry half of the chickpeas for 3 minutes. Remove with a slotted spoon. Drain on crumpled paper towel and repeat with the rest of the chickpeas. Partially cover the pan as some chickpeas may pop. Do not leave the oil unattended.

Reheat the oil and fry the chickpeas again in batches for 3 minutes each batch, or until browned. Drain. Season the paprika with the cayenne pepper and some salt, and sprinkle over the hot chickpeas. Leave to cool and serve.

PREPARATION TIME: 30 MINUTES +   COOKING TIME: 15 MINUTES

FRIED GREEN TOMATOES

90 g (3¹/₄ oz/³/₄ cup) plain (all-purpose) flour
¹/₂ teaspoon white pepper
35 g (1¹/₄ oz/¹/₄ cup) polenta
1 egg
185 ml (6 fl oz/³/₄ cup) milk
4 green tomatoes (about 500 g/1 lb 2 oz)
oil, for pan-frying

SERVES 4–6

Sift the flour, pepper and 1 teaspoon salt into a bowl. Add the polenta and stir to combine. Make a well in the centre.

Combine the egg and milk and add gradually to the flour mixture. Whisk the batter until just combined, but do not overbeat.

Cut the tomatoes into thick slices. Heat about 1 cm (¹/₂ inch) of oil in a frying pan.

Dip the tomatoes into the batter, drain the excess and fry for 1 minute on each side, turning only once with tongs. Drain on paper towel and serve immediately.

PREPARATION TIME: 15 MINUTES   COOKING TIME: 12 MINUTES

NOTE: Red tomatoes can also be used.

BHEL PURI

MINT CHUTNEY
50 g (1¾ oz) coriander (cilantro)
50 g (1¾ oz) mint
6 garlic cloves, chopped
3 red chillies, chopped
½ red onion, chopped
60 ml (2 fl oz/¼ cup) lemon juice

TAMARIND CHUTNEY
60 g (2¼ oz) fennel seeds
435 ml (15¼ fl oz/1¾ cups) tamarind purée
100 g (3½ oz) fresh ginger, sliced
300 g (10½ oz) grated palm sugar (jaggery) or soft brown sugar
1 teaspoon chilli powder
1 tablespoon ground cumin
1 tablespoon chaat masala (see Notes)
1 teaspoon black salt (see Notes)

3 all-purpose potatoes
1 tomato
120 g (4¼ oz) puffed rice (see Notes)
60 g (2¼ oz) sev noodles (see Notes)
1 green unripe mango, sliced into thin slivers
1 onion, finely chopped
4 tablespoons finely chopped coriander (cilantro) or mint leaves
1 teaspoon chaat masala
12 crushed puri crisps (see Notes)
coriander (cilantro) leaves, extra, to garnish

SERVES 6

To make the mint chutney, blend the ingredients together in a food processor or use a mortar and pestle. Transfer to a saucepan and bring to the boil. Remove from the heat, leave to cool, then season with salt.

To make the tamarind chutney, dry-fry the fennel seeds in a small frying pan over low heat until fragrant. Set aside. Mix together the tamarind purée, ginger and sugar with 250 ml (9 fl oz/1 cup) water in a saucepan. Cook over low heat until the tamarind blends into the mixture and the sugar completely dissolves.

Take out the ginger and cook the mixture to a thick pulp. Add the fennel seeds, chilli powder, ground cumin, chaat masala and black salt. Season with salt and reduce, stirring occasionally, over medium heat until thickened to a dropping consistency (it will fall in sheets off the spoon). Leave to cool.

To make the bhel puri, cook the potatoes in boiling water for 10 minutes, or until tender, then cut into small cubes. Score a cross in the base of the tomato. Put into a heatproof bowl and cover with boiling water. Leave for 30 seconds, then transfer to cold water, drain and peel away the skin from the cross. Cut the tomato in half, scoop out the seeds and roughly chop the flesh, reserving any juices.

Put the potato, tomato and reserved juice, puffed rice, sev noodles, mango, onion, chopped coriander, chaat masala and puri crisps in a large bowl and toss them together. When well mixed, stir in a little of each chutney. Vary the chutney amounts, depending on the flavour you want to achieve. The tamarind chutney has a tart flavour and the mint chutney is hot. Serve in small bowls and garnish with coriander leaves.

PREPARATION TIME: 40 MINUTES   COOKING TIME: 25 MINUTES

NOTES: Black salt, puffed rice, sev noodles, chaat masala and puri crisps are all available at Indian grocery stores.

Bhel puri is India's most famous chaat (snack), and is sold by street vendors who make up a mixture to suit your tastes.

MARINATED CHILLI MUSHROOMS

750 g (1 lb 10 oz) button mushrooms
500 ml (17 fl oz/2 cups) light olive oil
2 tablespoons lemon juice
1 garlic clove, finely chopped
$1/4$ teaspoon caster (superfine) sugar
1 red chilli, finely chopped
1 green chilli, finely chopped
1 tablespoon chopped coriander (cilantro)
1 tablespoon chopped flat-leaf
(Italian) parsley

SERVES 4–6

Wipe the mushrooms with damp paper towel to remove any dirt and put them in a bowl.

Mix together the oil, lemon juice, garlic, sugar and chilli. Pour over the mushrooms and mix well so that the mushrooms are evenly coated. Cover with plastic wrap and marinate for at least 30 minutes. Just before serving, add the herbs, then season and mix well.

PREPARATION TIME: 20 MINUTES +   COOKING TIME: NIL

CHICKPEA CHIPS

cooking oil spray
175 g (6 oz) besan (chickpea flour)
$1^{1}/2$ tablespoons olive oil
vegetable oil, for frying
freshly grated parmesan cheese,
to sprinkle (optional)

SERVES 6

Spray six saucers with cooking oil spray. Put the flour in a bowl and stir in 685 ml ($23^{1}/2$ fl oz/$2^{3}/4$ cups) cold water. Whisk with a wire whisk for about 2 minutes, or until smooth. Stir in the olive oil and season to taste.

Pour the mixture into a heavy-based saucepan and cook over low heat for about 8 minutes, stirring constantly, until thickened. Cook and stir until the mixture goes lumpy and starts to pull away from the sides of the pan. (This will take about 10–12 minutes.) Remove from the heat and beat until smooth. Working quickly before the mixture sets, distribute among the saucers and spread to an even thickness. Leave to cool and set.

Preheat the oven to 120°C (235°F/Gas $1/2$). Remove the mixture from the saucers and cut into sticks 5 cm (2 inches) long and 2 cm ($3/4$ inch) wide. Pour the vegetable oil into a large heavy-based saucepan to a depth of about 2.5 cm (1 inch). Heat to very hot and fry the sticks in batches until crisp and golden — about 2 minutes on each side. Remove with a slotted spoon and drain on crumpled paper towel. Transfer cooked batches to baking trays and keep warm in the oven while the rest are being fried. Serve hot, sprinkled with salt and freshly ground black pepper and grated parmesan.

PREPARATION TIME: 20 MINUTES +   COOKING TIME: 30 MINUTES

Marinated chilli mushrooms

VEGETABLE PAKORAS

RAITA
2 Lebanese (short) cucumbers, peeled, seeded and finely chopped
250 g (9 oz/1 cup) plain yoghurt
1 teaspoon ground cumin
1 teaspoon mustard seeds
$^1\!/_2$ teaspoon grated fresh ginger
paprika, to garnish

35 g (1$^1\!/_4$ oz/$^1\!/_3$ cup) besan (chickpea flour)
40 g (1$^1\!/_2$ oz/$^1\!/_3$ cup) self-raising flour
45 g (1$^3\!/_4$ oz/$^1\!/_3$ cup) soy flour
$^1\!/_2$ teaspoon ground turmeric
1 teaspoon cayenne pepper
$^1\!/_2$ teaspoon ground coriander
1 small green chilli, seeded and finely chopped
200 g (7 oz) cauliflower
140 g (5 oz) orange sweet potato
180 g (6$^1\!/_4$ oz) eggplant (aubergine)
180 g (6$^1\!/_4$ oz) asparagus, woody ends trimmed
oil, for deep-frying

SERVES 4

To make the raita, mix the cucumber and yoghurt in a bowl. Dry-fry the cumin and mustard seeds in a small frying pan over medium heat for 1 minute, or until fragrant and lightly browned, then add to the yoghurt mixture. Stir in the ginger, season to taste and mix together well. Garnish with paprika. Refrigerate until ready to serve.

Sift the besan, self-raising and soy flours into a bowl, then add the ground turmeric, cayenne pepper, ground coriander, chilli and 1 teaspoon salt. Gradually whisk in 250 ml (9 fl oz/1 cup) cold water until a batter forms. Set aside for 15 minutes. Preheat the oven to 120°C (235°F/Gas $^1\!/_2$).

Meanwhile, cut the cauliflower into small florets. Cut the orange sweet potato and eggplant into 5 mm ($^1\!/_4$ inch) slices, and cut the asparagus into 6 cm (2$^1\!/_2$ inch) lengths.

Fill a wok one-third full with oil and heat to 170°C (325°F), or until a cube of bread dropped in the oil browns in 20 seconds. Dip the vegetables in the batter, then deep-fry them in small batches, for 1–2 minutes, or until pale golden. Remove with a slotted spoon and drain on crumpled paper towel. Keep warm in the oven until all the vegetables are cooked. Serve with the raita.

PREPARATION TIME: 30 MINUTES +   COOKING TIME: 20 MINUTES

PUMPKIN AND HAZELNUT PESTO BITES

750 g (1 lb 10 oz) butternut pumpkin (squash)
30 ml (1 fl oz) oil
2 tablespoons freshly grated parmesan cheese (optional)

HAZELNUT PESTO
35 g (1¼ oz/¼ cup) roasted hazelnuts
35 g (1¼ oz) rocket (arugula)
1 tablespoon freshly grated parmesan cheese
30 ml (1 fl oz) oil

MAKES 48

Preheat the oven to 200°C (400°F/Gas 6). Peel the pumpkin and cut into 2 cm (¾ inch) slices, then cut into rough triangular shapes about 3 cm (1¼ inches) along the base. Toss with the oil and some salt and cracked black pepper until coated. Spread on a baking tray and bake for 35 minutes, or until cooked.

Meanwhile, to make the hazelnut pesto, process the hazelnuts, rocket, parmesan and oil, until they form a paste, then season to taste.

Spoon a small amount of the hazelnut pesto onto each piece of baked pumpkin and sprinkle with parmesan, if using, and some black pepper. Serve warm or cold.

PREPARATION TIME: 20 MINUTES   COOKING TIME: 35 MINUTES

ARTICHOKES WITH TARRAGON MAYONNAISE

4 medium globe artichokes
60 ml (2 fl oz/¼ cup) lemon juice

TARRAGON MAYONNAISE
1 egg yolk
1 tablespoon tarragon vinegar
½ teaspoon French mustard
170 ml (5½ fl oz/⅔ cup) olive oil

SERVES 4

Trim the stalks from the base of the artichokes. Using scissors, trim the points from the outer leaves. Using a sharp knife, cut the tops from the artichokes. Brush all cut areas of the artichokes with the lemon juice to prevent discolouration. Steam the artichokes for 30 minutes, or until tender, topping up the saucepan with boiling water if necessary. Remove from the heat and set aside to cool.

To make the tarragon mayonnaise, put the egg yolk, vinegar and mustard in a mixing bowl. Using a wire whisk, beat for 1 minute. At first, add the oil a teaspoon at a time, whisking constantly until the mixture is thick and creamy. As the mayonnaise thickens, pour the oil in a thin, steady stream. Continue whisking until all the oil is added, then season to taste. To serve, place a cooled artichoke on each plate with a little tarragon mayonnaise.

PREPARATION TIME: 30 MINUTES   COOKING TIME: 30 MINUTES

Pumpkin and hazelnut pesto bites

GRILLED VEGETABLES WITH GARLIC MAYONNAISE

2 eggplants (aubergines), cut into thin slices
4 small leeks, white part only
4 small zucchinis (courgettes)
2 red capsicums (peppers)
8 large flat mushrooms

DRESSING
1 tablespoon balsamic vinegar
2 tablespoons dijon mustard
2 teaspoons dried oregano leaves
250 ml (9 fl oz/1 cup) olive oil

GARLIC MAYONNAISE
2 egg yolks
1 tablespoon lemon juice
2 garlic cloves, crushed
250 ml (9 fl oz/1 cup) olive oil
1 tablespoon snipped chives
1 tablespoon chopped flat-leaf (Italian) parsley

SERVES 8

Sprinkle the eggplant with some salt and leave to stand for 30 minutes. Rinse under cold water, then pat dry with paper towel.

Halve the leeks and zucchinis lengthways. Cut the capsicum in half, remove the seeds and membrane and cut each half into four pieces.

To make the dressing, combine the vinegar, mustard and oregano in a bowl, then gradually whisk in the oil. Preheat the grill (broiler) to high.

Place the eggplant, leek, zucchini and capsicum in a single layer on a flat grill tray, then brush with some of the dressing. Cook under the grill on high for 5 minutes. Turn the vegetables once, brushing occasionally with dressing. Add the mushrooms, cap side up, to the grill tray and brush with the dressing. Continue cooking the vegetables for 10 minutes, or until tender, turning the mushrooms once. Brush the vegetables with dressing during cooking.

To make the mayonnaise, put the egg yolks, lemon juice and garlic in a food processor or blender and blend for 5 seconds until combined. With the motor running, add the oil slowly in a thin, steady stream until it is all added and the mayonnaise is thick and creamy. Add the chives, parsley and 1 tablespoon water and blend for 3 seconds until combined. Serve with the grilled vegetables.

PREPARATION TIME: 30 MINUTES   COOKING TIME: 15 MINUTES

NOTE: Garlic mayonnaise can be made several days ahead and refrigerated. Do not worry if the dressing separates — simply brush on as required.

OLIVE BASIL CHEESE SPREAD

250 g (9 oz/1 cup) cream cheese, softened
200 g (7 oz) feta cheese
20 g (³/₄ oz) basil leaves
60 ml (2 fl oz/¹/₄ cup) olive oil
15 Kalamata olives, pitted and roughly chopped
bruschetta, to serve

MAKES 500 G (1 LB 2 OZ/2 CUPS)

Combine the cream cheese, feta, basil, 1 tablespoon of the oil and ¹/₄ teaspoon cracked black pepper in a bowl and mix until smooth.

Fold in the olives and spoon into a serving bowl. Smooth the top with the back of the spoon and pour the remaining oil over the top. Garnish with a little more cracked pepper and serve with warm bruschetta.

PREPARATION TIME: 15 MINUTES   COOKING TIME: NIL

POTATO AND SAGE CHIPS

2 large all-purpose potatoes
2 tablespoons olive oil
25 sage leaves
salt, to sprinkle

SERVES 4–6

Preheat the oven to 200°C (400°F/Gas 6). Carefully cut the potatoes lengthways into paper-thin slices. Toss the slices in the oil.

Line two baking trays with baking paper. Sandwich a sage leaf between two slices of potato. Sprinkle with salt. Repeat to use all the potato. Bake for 25–30 minutes, or until browned and crisp, turning once during cooking.

PREPARATION TIME: 15 MINUTES   COOKING TIME: 30 MINUTES

NOTE: Some chips may take longer to cook than others. Watch them carefully to prevent them from burning.

Olive basil cheese spread

MARINATED ROASTED VEGETABLE DIP

1 small eggplant (aubergine)
2 zucchini (courgettes)
3 red capsicums (peppers)
125 ml (4 fl oz/^{1}/$_2$ cup) extra virgin olive oil
2 garlic cloves, sliced
2 roma (plum) tomatoes
200 g (7 oz) tinned artichoke hearts, drained
7 g (^{1}/$_4$ oz) oregano leaves
250 g (9 oz/1 cup) ricotta cheese
45 g (1^3/$_4$ oz/^{1}/$_4$ cup) black olives, pitted and sliced

SERVES 8

Slice the eggplant and zucchini. Put the slices in a colander over a bowl, sprinkle generously with some salt and leave for 15–20 minutes. Meanwhile, cut the red capsicums in half, remove the seeds and membrane and then cut into large flattish pieces. Cook, skin side up, under a hot grill (broiler) until the skin blackens and blisters. Cool in a plastic bag, then peel. Reserve about a quarter of the capsicum to use as a garnish and put the rest in a large non-metallic bowl.

Put half the olive oil in a bowl, then add half the garlic and a pinch of salt and mix. Rinse the eggplant and zucchini and pat dry with paper towel. Place the eggplant on a non-stick or foil-lined tray and brush with the garlic oil. Cook under a very hot grill for 4–6 minutes each side, or until golden brown, brushing both sides with oil during grilling. The eggplant will burn easily, so keep a close watch. Leave to cool while grilling the zucchini in the same way. Add both to the red capsicum in the bowl.

Slice the tomatoes lengthways, place on a non-stick or foil-lined baking tray and brush with the garlic oil. Reduce the temperature slightly and grill for 10–15 minutes, or until soft. Add to the bowl with the other vegetables.

Cut the artichokes into quarters and add to the bowl. Mix in any remaining garlic oil along with the remaining olive oil. Stir in the oregano and remaining garlic. Cover with a tight-fitting lid or plastic wrap and refrigerate for at least 2 hours.

Drain the vegetables and place in a food processor. Add the ricotta and process for 20 seconds, or until smooth. Reserve 1 tablespoon of the olives to garnish. Add the rest to the processor. Mix in a couple of short bursts — processing as coarsely or as finely as preferred — then transfer to a non-metallic bowl and cover with plastic wrap. Chill for at least 2 hours.

Slice the reserved roasted red capsicum into fine strips and arrange over the top of the dip with the reserved olives.

PREPARATION TIME: 55 MINUTES +   COOKING TIME: 50 MINUTES

IDLIS

220 g (7³/4 oz) urad dal
100 g (3¹/2 oz) rice flour (see Notes)
1 teaspoon fenugreek seeds

MAKES 20

Put the the dal in a bowl, cover with water and soak for at least 4 hours, or overnight.

Drain the dal, then grind in a food processor or blender with a little water, to form a fine paste.

Combine the rice flour, fenugreek seeds and 1 teaspoon salt in a large bowl and mix in enough water to make a thick, pourable batter. Mix the batters together. Cover with a cloth and leave in a warm place for 8 hours, until the batter ferments and bubbles. The batter will double in volume.

Pour the mixture into a greased idli mould, filling the cups almost full. Cover and steam the idlis over simmering water for 10–15 minutes, or until they are firm and puffed.

PREPARATION TIME: 10 MINUTES +   COOKING TIME: 30 MINUTES

NOTES: Traditionally, these are eaten with podi (see below), or as an accompaniment for dishes that have plenty of sauce.

For the best results, use rava-idli rice flour — it is a coarse flour suitable for making idlis.

PODI

110 g (3³/4 oz) urad dal
100 g (3¹/2 oz) chana dal
10 g (¹/4 oz) dried chillies
80 g (2³/4 oz/¹/2 cup) sesame seeds
¹/2 teaspoon sugar
1 tablespoon ghee

MAKES 220 G (7³/4 OZ)

Dry-fry the urad dal in a frying pan, stirring constantly until brown. Remove from the pan and repeat with the chana dal, dried chillies and sesame seeds. Grind the mixture to a powder with the sugar and ¹/2 teaspoon salt, using a spice grinder or mortar and pestle. Cool completely and store in a jar or an airtight container.

When ready to serve, heat the ghee in a frying pan and add 2 teaspoons of podi per person. Toss together until well mixed. Use as a dip or as a seasoning or eat it with idlis (see above).

PREPARATION TIME: 10 MINUTES   COOKING TIME: 10 MINUTES

SPINACH PIES

2 teaspoons dried yeast

1 teaspoon sugar

375 g (13 oz/3 cups) plain (all-purpose) flour

125 ml (4 fl oz/^{1}/$_2$ cup) olive oil

750 g (1 lb 10 oz) English spinach, trimmed

1 large onion, finely chopped

1 garlic clove, crushed

80 g (2^3/$_4$ oz/^{1}/$_2$ cup) pine nuts, toasted (see Note)

2 tablespoons lemon juice

1 teaspoon finely grated lemon zest

^{1}/$_4$ teaspoon ground nutmeg

MAKES ABOUT 20

Put the yeast and sugar in a bowl with 60 ml (2 fl oz/^{1}/$_4$ cup) warm water. Leave in a warm, draught-free place for 10 minutes, or until bubbles appear on the surface. The mixture should be frothy and slightly increased in volume. If your yeast doesn't foam, it is dead, so you will have to discard it and start again.

Sift the flour into a bowl, add the yeast mixture, 2 tablespoons of the olive oil and 185 ml (6 fl oz/^{3}/$_4$ cup) warm water. Mix to form a dough, then turn onto a lightly floured board and knead for 10 minutes until smooth and elastic. Put the dough in an oiled bowl and leave for up to 2 hours in a warm, draught-free place until doubled in size.

Preheat the oven to 190°C (375°F/Gas 5). Grease two large baking trays. Wash the spinach, leaving a generous amount of water on the leaves. Put in a saucepan, cover and cook over high heat until wilted. Transfer to a colander and squeeze against the sides to remove the excess water. Roughly chop the spinach.

Heat 1 tablespoon of the oil in a frying pan and cook the onion and garlic until softened. Put in a bowl with the spinach, pine nuts, lemon juice and zest. Season with the nutmeg and some salt and pepper. Set aside to cool.

Turn the dough onto a floured board and knock down. Divide into balls the size of an egg and roll each into a 10 cm (4 inch) round. Place 1 tablespoon of the filling in the centre of each round. Brush the edges of the rounds with water, then bring up the sides at three points to form a triangle, pressing the edges together to seal. Place on the trays, leaving room for the pies to spread as they cook. Brush them with beaten egg and bake for 15 minutes, or until golden. Serve hot.

PREPARATION TIME: 25 MINUTES   COOKING TIME: 20 MINUTES

NOTE: Toast the pine nuts in a dry frying pan over medium heat, stirring constantly, until they are golden brown and fragrant. Watch carefully as they will burn easily.

GRILLED TOMATOES WITH BRUSCHETTA

1 loaf Italian bread
4 large ripe tomatoes
½ teaspoon dried marjoram leaves
80 ml (2½ fl oz/⅓ cup) olive oil
2 tablespoons red wine vinegar
1 teaspoon soft brown sugar
1 garlic clove, halved
110 g (3¾ oz/½ cup) chopped, marinated artichokes
1 tablespoon finely chopped flat-leaf (Italian) parsley
sea salt, to sprinkle

SERVES 4

Cut the bread into thick slices. Preheat a grill (broiler). Cut the tomatoes in half and gently squeeze out the seeds. Place the tomatoes, cut side down, in a shallow, ovenproof dish. Combine the marjoram, oil, vinegar, sugar and some salt and pepper and mix well. Pour half over the tomatoes.

Cook the tomatoes under the hot grill for 30 minutes, turning halfway during cooking. Pour the remaining oil mixture over the tomatoes. Remove from the heat and keep warm.

Brush the bread slices liberally with some oil, on both sides, and toast until golden. Rub the cut surface of the garlic over the bread. Place the cooked tomatoes onto the bread, top with artichokes and sprinkle with parsley and sea salt.

PREPARATION TIME: 15 MINUTES   COOKING TIME: 35 MINUTES

POLENTA CHILLIES

330 g (11¾ oz) jar mild, whole chillies
60 g (2¼ oz/½ cup) grated cheddar cheese
100 g (3½ oz) soft cream cheese
40 g (1½ oz/⅓ cup) plain (all-purpose) flour
2 eggs, lightly beaten
110 g (3¾ oz/¾ cup) polenta
75 g (2¾ oz/¾ cup) dry breadcrumbs
oil, for deep-frying
sour cream, to serve (optional)

SERVES 6

Select twelve large, similar-sized chillies from the jar. Drain well and dry with paper towel. With a sharp knife, cut a slit down the length of one side of each chilli. Remove all the seeds and membrane. Combine the grated cheddar and cream cheese, then fill each chilli with the cheese mixture.

Put the flour onto a large plate and the beaten eggs in a small bowl. Combine the polenta and breadcrumbs in a small plastic bag, then transfer to a large plate. Roll each chilli in flour, shake off the excess, dip in the egg, then roll in the breadcrumb mixture to thoroughly coat the chillies. Refrigerate for 1 hour. Re-dip in the egg and re-roll in the breadcrumbs. Return to the refrigerator for 1 hour.

Fill a heavy-based saucepan one-third full of oil and heat the oil to 180°C (350°F), or until a cube of bread dropped into the oil browns in 15 seconds. Deep-fry the prepared chillies in small batches until golden and drain on paper towel. Serve with sour cream, if desired.

PREPARATION TIME: 30 MINUTES +   COOKING TIME: 12 MINUTES

Grilled tomatoes with bruschetta

VEGETARIAN STICKY RICE POCKETS

20 dried bamboo leaves (see Notes)

6 spring onions (scallions)

80 g (2³/4 oz/¹/2 cup) drained water chestnuts

400 g (14 oz) eggplant (aubergine)

125 ml (4 fl oz/¹/2 cup) oil

1 tablespoon mushroom soy sauce (see Notes)

3 small red chillies, seeded and finely chopped

2 teaspoons sugar

3 tablespoons chopped coriander (cilantro)

800 g (1 lb 12 oz/4 cups) white glutinous rice, washed and well drained

2 tablespoons soy sauce

1 teaspoon ground white pepper

MAKES 20

Soak the bamboo leaves in boiling water for 10 minutes, or until soft. Drain.

Meanwhile, chop the spring onions and water chestnuts and cut the eggplant into 1 cm (¹/2 inch) cubes.

Heat half the oil in a wok and swirl to coat the base and side. Cook the spring onion and eggplant over high heat for 4–5 minutes, or until golden. Stir in the water chestnuts, mushroom soy sauce, chilli, sugar and coriander. Leave to cool.

Bring 750 ml (26 fl oz/3 cups) water to a simmer in a saucepan. Heat the remaining oil in a separate saucepan, add the rice and stir for 2 minutes, or until coated. Stir in 125 ml (4 fl oz/¹/2 cup) of the hot water over low heat until it is all absorbed. Repeat until all the water has been added — this should take about 20 minutes. Add the soy sauce and white pepper.

Fold one end of a bamboo leaf on the diagonal to form a cone. Hold securely in one hand and spoon in 2 tablespoons of rice. Make an indent in the rice, add 1 tablespoon of the eggplant filling, then top with another tablespoon of rice. Fold the other end of the bamboo leaf over to enclose the filling, then secure with a toothpick. Tie tightly with kitchen string. Repeat with the remaining bamboo leaves, rice and filling.

Put the rice parcels in a single layer inside a double bamboo steamer. Cover with a lid and sit over a wok half filled with simmering water. Steam for 1¹/2 hours, or until the rice is tender, adding more boiling water to the wok as needed. Serve hot.

PREPARATION TIME: 1 HOUR +   COOKING TIME: 2 HOURS

NOTES: Bamboo leaves are used to wrap food prior to cooking, but they are not eaten.

Mushroom soy sauce is available from Asian food stores.

CRISPY CHEESE AND CURRY LENTIL BALLS

250 g (9 oz/1 cup) red lentils
4 spring onions (scallions)
1 large zucchini (courgette)
2 garlic cloves, crushed
1 teaspoon ground cumin
80 g (2³/4 oz/1 cup) fresh breadcrumbs
125 g (4¹/2 oz/1 cup) grated cheddar cheese
150 g (5¹/2 oz/1 cup) polenta
oil, for deep-frying

MAKES ABOUT 30

Put the lentils in a saucepan and cover with water. Bring to the boil, reduce the heat, cover and simmer for 10 minutes, or until tender. Drain.

Meanwhile, chop the spring onion and grate the zucchini.

Combine half the lentils in a food processor or blender with the spring onion and garlic. Process until smooth. Transfer to a large bowl, then stir in the remaining lentils, cumin, breadcrumbs, cheese and zucchini until well combined. Roll level teaspoons of the mixture into balls and toss lightly in the polenta to coat.

Fill a heavy-based saucepan one-third full of oil and heat the oil to 180°C (350°F), or until a cube of bread dropped into the oil browns in 15 seconds. Cook small batches of the lentil balls in the oil for 1 minute each batch, or until golden brown, crisp and heated through. Carefully remove with tongs or a slotted spoon and drain on crumpled paper towel. Serve hot.

PREPARATION TIME: 15 MINUTES   COOKING TIME: 20 MINUTES

CORN AND POTATO FRITTERS

2 large (all-purpose) potatoes
6 spring onions (scallions)
260 g (9¹/4 oz) tinned corn kernels, drained
4 eggs, lightly beaten
50 g (1³/4 oz/¹/2 cup) dry breadcrumbs
1 teaspoon garam masala
60 ml (2 fl oz/¹/4 cup) oil

DIPPING SAUCE
160 g (5³/4 oz/²/3 cup) plain yoghurt
2 tablespoons chopped mint leaves
2 teaspoons sweet chilli sauce

MAKES ABOUT 40

Roughly grate the potatoes. Drain on paper towel and squeeze out the excess moisture. Chop the spring onions. Combine the potato and spring onion in a bowl with the corn, egg, breadcrumbs and garam masala. Mix well.

Heat 2 tablespoons of the oil in a heavy-based frying pan. Cook heaped tablespoons of mixture over medium heat for 2 minutes each side, or until golden. Drain on crumpled paper towel and keep warm. Repeat until all the mixture is used, adding extra oil to the pan if necessary.

To make the dipping sauce, combine all the ingredients in a bowl. Serve with the fritters.

PREPARATION TIME: 15 MINUTES   COOKING TIME: 20 MINUTES

Crispy cheese and curry lentil balls

BAKED POLENTA
WITH SPICY RELISH

600 ml (21 fl oz) milk
100 g (3^1/$_2$ oz/^{2}/$_3$ cup) polenta (see Note)
25 g (1 oz) butter, diced
1 tablespoon olive oil
1 tablespoon polenta, extra

SPICY RELISH
2 red onions
500 g (1 lb 2 oz) roma (plum) tomatoes
1 tablespoon oil
1 large red chilli, finely chopped
^{1}/$_4$ teaspoon Mexican chilli powder,
or to taste
1 tablespoon soft brown sugar
1 tablespoon red wine vinegar

MAKES 48

Lightly grease a 20 x 30 cm (8 x 12 inch) cake tin. Bring the milk to the boil in a saucepan. Reduce the heat to medium and whisk in the polenta, pouring it in a stream, until it thickens. Stir continuously with a wooden spoon for 20 minutes, or until it leaves the side of the pan. Remove from the heat and stir in the butter. Season to taste.

Spread the polenta into the tin and smooth the top. Refrigerate for 2 hours, or until set.

To make the spicy tomato relish, roughly chop the onions and tomatoes. Heat the oil in a frying pan, add the onion and cook, stirring, over high heat, for 3 minutes. Add the tomato, chilli, chilli powder, sugar and vinegar. Simmer, stirring occasionally, for 20 minutes, or until thickened. Season with salt.

Preheat the oven to 200°C (400°F/Gas 6). Turn the polenta out onto a board, cut into 5 cm (2 inch) squares, then into triangles. Place on a baking tray covered with baking paper, brush with olive oil and sprinkle with the extra polenta. Bake for 10 minutes, or until the polenta is golden and has a crust. Serve hot or warm with the warm relish.

PREPARATION TIME: 20 MINUTES +   COOKING TIME: 1 HOUR

NOTE: You can also use instant polenta, which only takes about 3 minutes to cook.

POTATO AND CASHEW SAMOSAS

3 all-purpose potatoes
1 tablespoon olive oil
2 teaspoons chopped ginger
90 g (3¼ oz) roasted cashew nuts, chopped
15 g (½ oz/¼ cup) shredded coconut
60 ml (2 fl oz/¼ cup) coconut cream
3 tablespoons chopped coriander (cilantro) leaves
4 sheets shortcrust (pie) pastry
oil, for deep-frying

MAKES 16

Finely dice the potatoes. Heat the oil in a large heavy-based frying pan and cook the potatoes and ginger for 8 minutes over medium heat, stirring constantly. Add the cashews, shredded coconut, coconut cream and coriander, stir to combine and season. Leave to cool.

Cut each pastry sheet into four. Place quarter cupfuls of the filling in the centre of each square, then brush the edges of the pastry with water. Press the edges of the pastry together, twist to seal, then chill for 15 minutes.

Fill a large heavy-based saucepan one-third full of oil and heat the oil to 180°C (350°F), or until a cube of bread dropped into the oil browns in 15 seconds. Deep-fry the samosas in batches for 6 minutes, or until golden and crisp. Drain on paper towel and serve immediately with a dip made from plain yoghurt, finely chopped cucumber, chopped chilli and perhaps some chopped mint, if desired.

PREPARATION TIME: 20 MINUTES +   COOKING TIME: 40 MINUTES

EGGPLANT AND CAPSICUM GRILL

1 small eggplant (aubergine)
2 tablespoons oil
1 small onion
1 small red capsicum (pepper)
1 large focaccia (about 30 x 30 cm/ 12 x 12 inch)
90 g (3¼ oz/⅓ cup) tomato paste (concentrated purée)
3 tablespoons chopped coriander (cilantro) leaves
60 g (2¼ oz/½ cup) grated cheddar cheese
25 g (1 oz/¼ cup) shredded parmesan cheese

SERVES 4

Cut the eggplant into 1 cm (½ inch) slices. Heat the oil in a large frying pan. Cook the eggplant slices for 2 minutes, or until soft and just golden. Drain on paper towel.

Finely slice the onion. Cut the red capsicum in half, remove the seeds and membrane and cut into thin strips.

Cut the focaccia into four squares, then in half horizontally. Toast each side until golden and spread with the tomato paste.

Layer the eggplant, onion, red capsicum, coriander and the combined cheeses on each square. Place under a moderately hot grill (broiler) for 2–3 minutes, or until the cheese has melted. Serve immediately.

PREPARATION TIME: 20 MINUTES   COOKING TIME: 8 MINUTES

Potato and cashew samosas

MUSHROOMS WITH HERB NUT BUTTER

12 large mushrooms
1 tablespoon olive oil
1 small onion, finely chopped
40 g (1$\frac{1}{2}$ oz) blanched almonds
1 garlic clove, chopped
1 tablespoon lemon juice
3 tablespoons parsley sprigs
3 teaspoons chopped thyme or
1 teaspoon dried thyme
3 teaspoons chopped rosemary or
1 teaspoon dried rosemary
1 tablespoon snipped chives
75 g (2$\frac{3}{4}$ oz) butter, chopped

SERVES 4–6

Preheat the oven to 180°C (350°F/Gas 4). Brush a shallow ovenproof dish with a little oil or melted butter. Remove the stalks from the mushrooms and finely chop the stalks. Heat the oil in a small frying pan, then add the onion. Cook over medium heat for 2–3 minutes, or until soft and golden. Add the chopped mushroom stalks. Cook for 2 minutes, or until softened. Remove from the heat.

Put the almonds, garlic, lemon juice, parsley, thyme, rosemary, chives, butter, $\frac{1}{2}$ teaspoon salt and $\frac{1}{4}$ teaspoon pepper in a food processor. Process for 20–30 seconds, or until the mixture is smooth.

Place the mushroom caps in the ovenproof dish. Spoon equal amounts of the onion and mushroom mixture into each cap and smooth the surface. Top each mushroom with the almond and herb mixture. Bake for 10–15 minutes, or until the mushrooms are cooked through and the butter has melted.

PREPARATION TIME: 20 MINUTES   COOKING TIME: 20 MINUTES

NOTE: Mushrooms are best cooked just before serving. Assemble the caps up to 2 hours before serving and store, covered, on a flat tray, in the refrigerator.

POTATO AND HERB FRITTERS

620 g (1 lb 6 oz/4 cups) finely grated potato
185 g (6½ oz/1½ cups) finely grated sweet potato
3 tablespoons finely snipped chives
1 tablespoon finely chopped oregano
2 tablespoons finely chopped flat-leaf (Italian) parsley
2 eggs, lightly beaten
30 g (1 oz/¼ cup) plain (all-purpose) flour
1 tablespoon olive oil
250 g (9 oz/1 cup) light sour cream
dill sprigs, to garnish

SERVES 4–6

Combine the potato and sweet potato with the chives, oregano, parsley, egg and sifted flour in a bowl. Stir with a wooden spoon until all the ingredients are just combined.

Heat the oil in heavy-based frying pan. Spoon heaped tablespoons of the mixture into the pan. Cook over medium–high heat for 4 minutes each side, or until golden. Serve warm, topped with sour cream and dill sprigs.

PREPARATION TIME: 25 MINUTES   COOKING TIME: 8 MINUTES

BLACK OLIVE AND CAPSICUM TAPENADE

75 g (2¾ oz) pitted black olives, sliced
75 g (2¾ oz) sun-dried capsicums (peppers) in oil, drained
1 tablespoon capers
1 large garlic clove
30 g (1 oz) flat-leaf (Italian) parsley
1 tablespoon lime juice
90 ml (3 fl oz) extra virgin olive oil

MAKES ABOUT 250 ML (9 FL OZ/1 CUP)

Blend the olives, sun-dried capsicums, capers, garlic and parsley together in a food processor or blender until finely minced. With the motor running, slowly add the lime juice and olive oil and process until just combined.

Transfer to a sterilized jar, seal and refrigerate for up to 2 weeks. Return to room temperature before serving.

Serve on bread or crackers, either as a spread by itself or spooned on top of ricotta cheese.

PREPARATION TIME: 15 MINUTES   COOKING TIME: NIL

Potato and herb fritters

HERBED CHEESE CRACKERS

BISCUIT PASTRY

125 g (4$\frac{1}{2}$ oz/1 cup) plain (all-purpose) flour
$\frac{1}{2}$ teaspoon baking powder
60 g (2$\frac{1}{4}$ oz) butter
1 egg, lightly beaten
60 g (2$\frac{1}{4}$ oz) cheddar cheese, grated
1 teaspoon snipped chives
1 teaspoon chopped flat-leaf (Italian) parsley (see Note)
1 tablespoon iced water

CHEESE FILLING

80 g (2$\frac{3}{4}$ oz) cream cheese, softened
20 g ($\frac{3}{4}$ oz) butter
1 tablespoon snipped chives
1 tablespoon chopped flat-leaf (Italian) parsley (see Note)
$\frac{1}{4}$ teaspoon lemon pepper
90 g (3$\frac{1}{4}$ oz) cheddar cheese, grated

SERVES 4–6

Preheat the oven to 190°C (375°F/Gas 5). Line two baking trays with baking paper.

To make the biscuit pastry, sift the flour and baking powder into a large bowl and add the chopped butter. Rub in the butter with your fingertips, until the mixture resembles fine breadcrumbs.

Make a well in the centre and add the egg, cheese, herbs and iced water. Mix with a flat-bladed knife, using a cutting action, until the mixture comes together in beads. Gently gather together and lift out onto a lightly floured surface. Press together into a ball.

Roll the pastry between sheets of baking paper to 3 mm ($\frac{1}{8}$ inch) thick. Remove the top sheet of paper and cut the pastry into rounds, using a 5 cm (2 inch) cutter. Place the rounds onto the baking trays. Re-roll the remaining pastry and repeat the cutting process. Bake for about 8 minutes, or until lightly browned. Transfer to a wire rack to cool.

To make the filling, beat the cream cheese and butter in a small bowl using electric beaters until light and creamy. Add the herbs, pepper and cheese and beat until smooth. Spread $\frac{1}{2}$ teaspoon of filling on half of the biscuits and sandwich together with the remaining biscuits.

PREPARATION TIME: 40 MINUTES   COOKING TIME: 16 MINUTES

NOTES: You can use chopped lemon thyme instead of parsley.

The biscuits can be made 2 days ahead and stored in an airtight container, or frozen. The filling can be made a day ahead and stored, covered, in the refrigerator.

BEETROOT HUMMUS

250 g (9 oz) dried chickpeas
1 large onion
500 g (1 lb 2 oz) beetroot (beets)
125 ml (4 fl oz/$\frac{1}{2}$ cup) tahini
3 garlic cloves, crushed
60 ml (2 oz/$\frac{1}{4}$ cup) lemon juice
1 tablespoon ground cumin
60 ml (2 oz/$\frac{1}{4}$ cup) olive oil

SERVES 8

Put the chickpeas in a large bowl, cover with cold water and soak overnight. Drain.

Chop the onion. Put the chickpeas and onion in a large heavy-based saucepan, cover with water and bring to the boil. Cook for 1 hour, or until the chickpeas are very soft. Drain, reserving 250 ml (9 fl oz/1 cup) of the cooking liquid. Leave to cool.

Cook the beetroot in a large saucepan of boiling water until tender. Drain and leave to cool slightly before removing the skins.

Chop the beetroot and put in a food processor, in batches if necessary. Add the chickpea and onion mixture, tahini, garlic, lemon juice and cumin and process until smooth. Slowly add the reserved cooking liquid and olive oil while the motor is running. Process until the mixture is thoroughly combined. Drizzle with a little olive oil and serve with pitta bread.

PREPARATION TIME: 25 MINUTES +   COOKING TIME: 1 HOUR 15 MINUTES

CAULIFLOWER FRITTERS

600 g (1 lb 5 oz) cauliflower
55 g (2 oz/$\frac{1}{2}$ cup) besan (chickpea flour)
2 teaspoons ground cumin
1 teaspoon ground coriander
1 teaspoon ground turmeric
pinch cayenne pepper
1 egg, lightly beaten
1 egg yolk
oil, for deep-frying

MAKES ABOUT 40 PIECES

Cut the cauliflower into bite-sized florets. Sift the flour and spices into a bowl, then stir in $\frac{1}{2}$ teaspoon salt and make a well in the centre.

Combine 60 ml (2 fl oz/$\frac{1}{4}$ cup) water with the egg and egg yolk and gradually pour into the well, whisking to make a smooth batter. Cover and leave for 30 minutes.

Fill a deep heavy-based saucepan one-third full of oil and heat to 180°C (350°F), or until a cube of bread dropped into the oil browns in 15 seconds. Holding the cauliflower florets by the stem, dip into the batter, draining the excess back into the bowl. Deep-fry in batches for 3–4 minutes, or until puffed and brown. Drain, season and serve hot.

PREPARATION TIME: 15 MINUTES +   COOKING TIME: 15 MINUTES

Beetroot hummus

LENTIL AND CHICKPEA BURGERS WITH CORIANDER GARLIC CREAM

250 g (9 oz/1 cup) red lentils

1 tablespoon oil

2 onions, sliced

1 tablespoon tandoori mix powder

425 g (15 oz) tinned chickpeas, drained

1 tablespoon grated fresh ginger

1 egg

3 tablespoons chopped flat-leaf (Italian) parsley

2 tablespoons chopped coriander (cilantro)

180 g (6¹/₂ oz/2¹/₄ cups) stale breadcrumbs

flour, to dust

CORIANDER GARLIC CREAM

125 g (4¹/₂ oz/¹/₂ cup) sour cream

125 ml (4 fl oz/¹/₂ cup) pouring (whipping) cream

1 garlic clove, crushed

2 tablespoons chopped coriander (cilantro)

2 tablespoons chopped flat-leaf (Italian) parsley

MAKES 10 BURGERS

Prepare and heat a barbecue grill or hotplate. Bring a large saucepan of water to the boil. Add the lentils to the boiling water and simmer, uncovered, for 10 minutes, or until the lentils are tender. Drain well. Heat the oil in a frying pan and cook the onion until tender. Add the tandoori mix and stir until fragrant. Cool the mixture slightly.

Place the chickpeas, half of the lentils, ginger, egg, and onion mixture in a food processor. Process for 20 seconds, or until smooth. Transfer to a bowl. Stir in the remaining lentils, parsley, coriander and breadcrumbs, and combine well. Divide the mixture into 10 portions.

Shape the portions into round patties. (If the mixture is too soft, refrigerate for 15 minutes, or until firm.) Toss them in flour and shake off any excess. Place the patties on the lightly greased barbecue. Cook for 3–4 minutes on each side, or until browned, turning once. Serve with the coriander garlic cream.

To make the coriander garlic cream, combine all of the ingredients in a bowl and mix well.

PREPARATION TIME: 30 MINUTES +   COOKING TIME: 30 MINUTES

NOTES: The patties can be prepared up to 2 days ahead and stored, covered, in the refrigerator. If you prefer, you can cook the patties in a frying pan brushed lightly with oil.

The coriander garlic cream can be made up to 3 days in advance. Place in a covered container and store in the refrigerator.

PARMESAN AND PESTO TOASTS

1 baguette
16 large sun-dried tomatoes
150 g (5$\frac{1}{2}$ oz) parmesan cheese, thinly shaved

PESTO
50 g (1$\frac{3}{4}$ oz) basil leaves
2 tablespoons snipped chives
50 g (1$\frac{3}{4}$ oz/$\frac{1}{3}$ cup) pine nuts
2–3 garlic cloves
60 ml (2 fl oz/$\frac{1}{4}$ cup) olive oil

SERVES 8–10

Freeze the baguette until firm. Cut it into very thin slices, using a sharp serrated knife. Toast the slices under a hot grill (broiler) until they are golden brown on both sides. Cut the sun-dried tomatoes into thin strips.

To make the pesto, put all of the ingredients in a food processor. Process for 20–30 seconds, or until smooth.

Spread the pesto mixture evenly over the toasted baguette slices. Top with strips of sun-dried tomato and shavings of parmesan cheese.

PREPARATION TIME: 30 MINUTES   COOKING TIME: 5 MINUTES

STEAMED RICE DUMPLINGS

400 g (14 oz/2 cups) long-grain rice
4 pieces banana leaf
(each 14 x 25 cm/5$\frac{1}{2}$ x 10 inches)
(see Note)

SERVES 4

Rinse the rice under cold running water, then drain. Put in a saucepan with 500 ml (17 fl oz/2 cups) water and bring to the boil. Reduce the heat to low and simmer for 5 minutes, or until all the water has been absorbed. Allow the rice to cool.

Lightly oil the pieces of banana leaf and divide the cooled rice among them. Form the rice into a log along the long side of the leaf, then roll up to enclose the rice. Secure the ends with string or toothpicks.

Bring a large saucepan of water to the boil, add the rice packages, cover and simmer over medium heat for 2 hours. Top up with boiling water occasionally to keep the packages afloat. Remove the packages, then refrigerate until cold and firm. Unwrap before serving.

PREPARATION TIME: 5 MINUTES +   COOKING TIME: 2 HOURS 15 MINUTES

NOTE: If you can't find banana leaves, use pieces of clean, unbleached calico.

Parmesan and pesto toasts

PIROZHKI

310 g (11 oz/2$^1/_2$ cups) plain (all-purpose) flour
180 g (6$^1/_4$ oz) cold butter, cut into cubes
1 egg yolk
60 g (2$^1/_4$ oz/$^1/_4$ cup) sour cream

FILLING
150 g (5$^1/_2$ oz) mushrooms
50 g (1$^3/_4$ oz) butter
1 small onion, finely chopped
95 g (3$^1/_2$ oz/$^1/_2$ cup) cooked short-grain rice
1 hard-boiled egg, finely chopped
2 tablespoons finely chopped flat-leaf (Italian) parsley
2 tablespoons finely chopped dill
1 egg, lightly beaten

MAKES ABOUT 20

Sift the flour and $^1/_2$ teaspoon salt into a large bowl and add the butter. Using your fingertips, rub the butter into the flour until the mixture resembles fine breadcrumbs. Add the combined egg yolk and sour cream. Mix with a flat-bladed knife, using a cutting action, to form a dough, adding up to 1 tablespoon water, if necessary.

Turn onto a lightly floured surface and gather together into a smooth ball. (Do not knead or you will have tough pastry.) Cover with plastic wrap and refrigerate for 30 minutes.

To make the filling, process the mushrooms in a food processor until finely chopped. Melt the butter in a frying pan, then cook the onion for 3 minutes, or until softened but not brown. Add the chopped mushrooms and cook, stirring, for a further 3 minutes. Stir in the rice. Transfer to a bowl and leave to cool. Stir in the chopped egg and herbs and season well.

Preheat the oven to 190°C (375°F/Gas 5). Roll out the pastry thinly, half at a time, on a floured surface. Cut 20 rounds, with an 8 cm (3$^1/_4$ inch) plain cutter. Put 1 tablespoon of filling in the centre of each round. Brush the pastry edges with the beaten egg, fold in half and pinch the edges to seal. Prick the tops with a fork. Put on a baking tray and refrigerate for 30 minutes. Brush the pastries with egg and bake for 15 minutes, or until golden. Serve hot.

PREPARATION TIME: 50 MINUTES +   COOKING TIME: 25 MINUTES

NACHOS WITH GUACAMOLE

440 g (15½ oz) tinned red kidney beans, rinsed and drained
90 g (3¼ oz/⅓ cup) ready-made tomato salsa
250 g (9 oz) corn chips
250 g (9 oz/2 cups) grated cheddar cheese
375 g (13 oz/1½ cups) ready-made tomato salsa, extra
90 g (3¼ oz/⅓ cup) sour cream

GUACAMOLE
1 spring onion (scallion)
1 small tomato
1 large avocado
1 tablespoon lemon juice

SERVES 4

Preheat the oven to 180°C (350°F/Gas 4). Combine the kidney beans and salsa, then divide the mixture between four ovenproof serving plates. Cover with corn chips and grated cheese. Put in the oven for 3–5 minutes, or until the cheese has melted.

To assemble, spoon the extra salsa onto the melted cheese, then top with guacamole and sour cream.

To make the guacamole, finely chop the spring onion and tomato. Cut the avocado in half, discard the skin and stone. Mash the flesh lightly with a fork and combine with the spring onion, tomato, lemon juice and some freshly ground pepper.

PREPARATION TIME: 20 MINUTES   COOKING TIME: 5 MINUTES

ONION BHAJI

4 large onions
80 g (2¾ oz/¾ cup) besan (chickpea flour)
60 g (2¼ oz/½ cup) plain (all-purpose) flour
1½ teaspoons bicarbonate of soda (baking soda)
1 teaspoon chilli powder
1 egg, lightly beaten
4 garlic cloves, chopped
oil, for pan-frying

SERVES 6–8

Cut the onions in half and thinly slice. Sift the flours, bicarbonate of soda and chilli powder into a bowl. Make a well in the centre, add the combined egg and 310 ml (10¾ fl oz/1¼ cups) water and stir to make a smooth creamy batter, adding a little more water if necessary. Add the onion and garlic and mix well.

Heat the oil, about 1 cm (½ inch) deep, in a wide, flat frying pan. Drop in tablespoons of the mixture and press into patties. Fry the bhaji on both sides until golden brown and cooked through, then drain on paper towel. Serve hot with chilli sauce or mango chutney.

PREPARATION TIME: 20 MINUTES   COOKING TIME: 15 MINUTES

NOTE: For a milder taste, use sweet paprika instead of chilli powder.

SPRING ROLLS

4 dried Chinese mushrooms
150 g (5½ oz) fried tofu
1 large carrot
70 g (2½ oz) water chestnuts
6 spring onions (scallions)
150 g (5½ oz) Chinese cabbage (wong bok)
1 tablespoon oil
2 garlic cloves, crushed
1 tablespoon grated fresh ginger
1 tablespoon soy sauce
white pepper, to taste
1 tablespoon cornflour (cornstarch)
10 large spring roll wrappers
oil, extra, for deep-frying

MAKES 20

Soak the dried mushrooms in boiling water for 20 minutes. Drain and squeeze to remove any excess liquid. Slice the mushroom caps and discard the hard stems.

Cut the tofu into fine strips and cut the carrot into very fine batons. Chop the water chestnuts and spring onions and shred the Chinese cabbage.

Heat the oil in a large wok, swirling gently to coat the base and side. Stir-fry the garlic, ginger, tofu, carrot and water chestnuts for 30 seconds, over high heat. Add the spring onion and Chinese cabbage and cook for 1 minute, or until the cabbage is just softened. Add the soy sauce and some salt, white pepper and sugar, to taste, then allow to cool. Add the sliced mushroom caps.

Mix the cornflour with 2 tablespoons water to form a paste. Keep the spring roll wrappers covered with a clean damp tea towel (dish towel) while you work. Place two wrappers on a board, one on top of the other. (The rolls are made with two layers of wrappers.) Cut the large square into four squares. Brush the edges of each square with a little cornflour paste. Place about 1 tablespoon of the filling in the centre of one square. With a corner facing you, roll up the wrapper firmly, folding in the sides as you roll. Repeat with the remaining wrappers and filling.

Fill a deep heavy-based saucepan one-third full of oil and heat the oil to 180°C (350°F), or until a cube of bread dropped into the oil browns in 15 seconds. Deep-fry the spring rolls, about four at a time, for 3 minutes, or until golden. Drain on crumpled paper towel.

PREPARATION TIME: 45 MINUTES +   COOKING TIME: 20 MINUTES

AVOCADO WITH LIME AND CHILLIES

2 ripe avocados
1 teaspoon finely grated lime zest
2 tablespoons lime juice
1 teaspoon soft brown sugar
1 tablespoon olive oil
1 tablespoon chopped flat-leaf (Italian) parsley
2–3 jalapeño chillies, seeded and diced

SERVES 6

Peel and slice the avocados.

Thoroughly combine the lime zest and juice, sugar, oil, parsley and chillies in a small bowl. Pour over the sliced avocado and serve.

PREPARATION TIME: 20 MINUTES   COOKING TIME: NIL

NOTE: The lime juice prevents the avocados browning. Lemon juice may be substituted.

CRUNCHY STUFFED TOFU PUFFS

12 deep-fried tofu puffs (see Note)
90 g (3^1/$_4$ oz/1 cup) bean sprouts, trimmed
40 g (1^1/$_2$ oz/^{1}/$_4$ cup) roasted peanuts, chopped
1 carrot, grated
1 tablespoon chopped coriander (cilantro) leaves

CHILLI SAUCE
2 small red chillies, finely chopped
2 garlic cloves, crushed
2 teaspoons soft brown sugar
1 tablespoon soy sauce
1 tablespoon vinegar
125 ml (4 fl oz/^{1}/$_2$ cup) boiling water

SERVES 6–8

Cut the tofu puffs in half. Cut a small slit in each half and open it up carefully to form a pocket.

Place the bean sprouts, peanuts, carrot and coriander in a bowl, and toss until well mixed. Fill each pocket with a portion of the mixture. Serve drizzled with a little chilli sauce, and offer the rest of the sauce for dipping.

To make the sauce, combine all the ingredients in a small saucepan, bring to the boil, reduce the heat and simmer for 5 minutes, or until the sauce thickens slightly.

PREPARATION TIME: 30 MINUTES   COOKING TIME: 5 MINUTES

NOTE: Tofu puffs are cubes of tofu that have been deep-fried and are puffed and golden. They are available from Asian food stores.

CHILLI PUFFS WITH CURRIED VEGETABLES

CHOUX PASTRY

90 g (3¼ oz) butter

155 g (5½ oz/1¼ cups) plain (all-purpose) flour, sifted

¼ teaspoon chilli powder

4 eggs, lightly beaten

CURRIED VEGETABLES

4 yellow squash

100 g (3½ oz) snow peas (mangetout)

1 carrot

2 onions

50 g (1¾ oz) butter

2 tablespoons mild curry paste

300 g (10½ oz) small oyster mushrooms

1 tablespoon lemon juice

MAKES 12

Preheat the oven to 210°C (415°F/Gas 6–7). Sprinkle two 28 x 32 cm (11¼ x 12¾ inch) baking trays with water.

To make the choux pastry, combine the butter and 310 ml (10¾ fl oz/1¼ cups) water in a saucepan. Stir over low heat for 5 minutes, or until the butter melts and the mixture comes to the boil. Remove from the heat, add the flour and chilli powder all at once and stir with a wooden spoon until just combined.

Return the pan to the heat and beat constantly over low heat for 3 minutes, or until the mixture thickens and comes away from the sides and base of the pan. Transfer the mixture to a large bowl. Using electric beaters, beat the mixture on high speed for 1 minute. Add the egg gradually, beating until the mixture is stiff and glossy. (This stage could take up to 5 minutes.)

Place the choux pastry mixture, in mounds measuring about 2 tablespoons each, onto the prepared trays, spacing them about 10 cm (4 inches) apart. Sprinkle with a little water and bake for 20 minutes. Reduce the heat to 180°C (350°F/Gas 4) and bake for 50 minutes, or until the puffs are crisp and well browned. (Cut a small slit into each puff halfway through cooking to allow any excess steam to escape and the puff to dry out.) Transfer the puffs to a wire rack to cool.

To make the curried vegetables, thinly slice the squash. Cut the snow peas in half diagonally. Cut the carrot into thin strips and slice the onions. Heat the butter in a frying pan and add the onions. Cook over low heat for 5 minutes, or until golden, then stir in the curry paste. Add the mushrooms and the other vegetables and stir over high heat for 1 minute. Add the lemon juice, remove from the heat and stir. Cut the puffs in half and remove any uncooked mixture from the centre with a spoon. Fill with the vegetables. Serve immediately.

PREPARATION TIME: 35 MINUTES   COOKING TIME: 1 HOUR 5 MINUTES

BAKED RICOTTA

2 kg (4 lb 8 oz) whole ricotta cheese
185 ml (6 fl oz/³/₄ cup) olive oil
185 ml (6 fl oz/³/₄ cup) lemon juice
2 tablespoons thin strips lemon zest
2 garlic cloves, crushed
25 g (1 oz) finely shredded basil leaves
50 g (1³/₄ oz/¹/₃ cup) semi-dried
(sun-blushed) tomatoes, roughly
chopped
Italian-style bread or bruschetta, to serve

SERVES 8–10

Remove any paper from the base of the ricotta and put the ricotta in a plastic colander. Place over a bowl, ensuring the base of the colander is not touching the base of the bowl. Cover with plastic wrap and leave overnight in the refrigerator, to drain.

Preheat the oven to 250°C (500°F/Gas 9). Line a baking tray with baking paper. Transfer the ricotta to the tray and brush with a little of the olive oil. Bake for 30 minutes, or until golden brown. Allow to cool slightly.

Mix the remaining olive oil, lemon juice and zest, garlic and basil in a bowl and season to taste. Place the whole ricotta on a platter, pour on the dressing and scatter with the semi-dried tomatoes. Serve with thin slices of Italian-style bread or bruschetta.

PREPARATION TIME: 15 MINUTES + COOKING TIME: 30 MINUTES

POTATO BASKETS WITH CHEESE

20 small new potatoes, unpeeled
250 g (9 oz/1 cup) ricotta cheese
35 g (1¹/₄ oz) cheddar cheese, grated
25 g (1 oz) parmesan cheese, shredded
oil, to spray or brush
15 g (¹/₂ oz) chives, finely snipped,
to garnish

MAKES ABOUT 40

Preheat the oven to 200°C (400°F/Gas 6). Boil or steam the potatoes for 10 minutes, or until just tender when tested with a skewer (do not overcook or the potatoes will fall apart when you are preparing them). Drain well and cool completely. Meanwhile, in a small bowl combine the ricotta, cheddar and parmesan. Season to taste and set aside.

Cut the cooled potatoes in half and use a melon baller to scoop out the flesh, leaving a 5 mm (¹/₄ inch) border. Discard the flesh. Lightly spray the potato halves with oil and bake on baking trays for 30–45 minutes, or until crisp and golden. Heat the grill (broiler) to high. Fill each potato shell with 1 teaspoon of the cheese mixture and grill for 5–8 minutes, or until the tops are lightly golden and the cheese has melted. Arrange on a serving dish and garnish each with snipped chives. Serve immediately.

PREPARATION TIME: 15 MINUTES COOKING TIME: 55 MINUTES

NOTE: The potatoes can be cooked and filled in advance, then grilled just before serving.

Baked ricotta

VEGETARIAN DOLMADES

6 spring onions (scallions)
125 ml (4 fl oz/$^1/_2$ cup) olive oil
150 g (5$^1/_2$ oz/$^3/_4$ cup) long-grain rice
15 g ($^1/_2$ oz) chopped mint
2 tablespoons chopped dill
170 ml (5$^1/_2$ fl oz/$^2/_3$ cup) lemon juice
35 g (1$^1/_4$ oz/$^1/_4$ cup) currants
40 g (1$^1/_2$ oz/$^1/_4$ cup) pine nuts
235 g (8$^1/_2$ oz) packaged vine leaves
(about 50)
2 tablespoons olive oil, extra

MAKES ABOUT 50

Chop the spring onions. Heat the oil in a saucepan. Add the spring onion and cook over medium heat for 1 minute. Stir in the rice, mint, dill and half the lemon juice. Season to taste. Add 250 ml (9 fl oz/1 cup) water and bring to the boil, then reduce the heat, cover and simmer for 20 minutes. Remove the lid, fork through the currants and pine nuts, cover with a paper towel, then the lid and leave to cool.

Rinse the vine leaves and gently separate. Drain, then dry on paper towel. Trim any thick stems with scissors. Line the base of a 20 cm (8 inch) saucepan with any torn or misshapen leaves. Choose the larger leaves for filling and use the smaller leaves to patch up any gaps.

Place a leaf, shiny side down. Spoon a tablespoon of filling into the centre, bring in the sides and roll up tightly from the stem end. Place, seam side down, with the stem end closest to you, in the base of the pan, arranging them close together in a single layer.

Pour in the rest of the lemon juice, the extra oil and about 185 ml (6 fl oz/ $^3/_4$ cup) water to just cover the dolmades. Cover with an inverted plate and place a tin on the plate to firmly compress the dolmades and keep them in place while they are cooking. Cover with the lid.

Bring to the boil, then reduce the heat and simmer for 45 minutes. Cool in the pan. Serve at room temperature.

PREPARATION TIME: 1 HOUR +   COOKING TIME: 1 HOUR 15 MINUTES

NOTE: Store, covered with the cooking liquid, in the refrigerator for up to 2 weeks.

SALADS AND SIDES

WARM LENTIL AND RICE SALAD

185 g (6½ oz/1 cup) green lentils
200 g (7 oz/1 cup) basmati rice
4 large red onions
4 garlic cloves, crushed
250 ml (9 fl oz/1 cup) olive oil
45 g (1¾ oz) butter
3 spring onions (scallions)
2 teaspoons ground cinnamon
2 teaspoons ground sweet paprika
2 teaspoons ground cumin
2 teaspoons ground coriander

SERVES 6

Cook the lentils and rice in separate saucepans of water until the grains are just tender, then drain.

Meanwhile, finely slice the onions. Cook the onion and garlic in the oil and butter for 30 minutes, over low heat, until very soft. Chop the spring onions and set aside until ready to use.

Stir in the cinnamon, paprika, cumin and coriander and cook for a few minutes longer.

Combine the onion and spice mixture with the well-drained rice and lentils. Stir in the chopped spring onions until combined and add freshly ground black pepper to taste. Serve warm.

PREPARATION TIME: 15 MINUTES   COOKING TIME: 40 MINUTES

NOTES: Do not use red lentils for this recipe as they become mushy very quickly and do not retain their shape.

It is not necessary to soak the lentils prior to cooking, but they need to be rinsed thoroughly.

TUNISIAN CARROT SALAD

500 g (1 lb 2 oz) carrots
3 tablespoons finely chopped flat-leaf (Italian) parsley
1 teaspoon ground cumin
80 ml (2½ fl oz/⅓ cup) olive oil
60 ml (2 fl oz/¼ cup) red wine vinegar
2 garlic cloves, crushed
¼–½ teaspoon ready-made harissa (see Notes)
12 black olives
2 hard-boiled eggs, quartered

SERVES 6

Thinly slice the carrots. Bring 500 ml (17 fl oz/2 cups) water to the boil in a saucepan. Add the carrot and cook until tender. Drain and transfer to a bowl. Add the parsley, cumin, olive oil, vinegar and garlic. Season with the harissa and some salt and pepper. Stir well.

Put the carrots in a serving dish and garnish with the olives and egg.

PREPARATION TIME: 10 MINUTES   COOKING TIME: 10 MINUTES

NOTES: If the carrots are not sweet, add a little honey to the dressing.
    Harissa is a spicy paste blend available from delicatessens.

HERBED FETA SALAD

2 slices thick white bread
200 g (7 oz) feta cheese
1 garlic clove, crushed
1 tablespoon finely chopped marjoram
1 tablespoon finely snipped chives
1 tablespoon finely chopped basil
2 tablespoons white wine vinegar
80 ml (2½ fl oz/⅓ cup) olive oil
1 red coral lettuce
1 butter, coral or oak-leaf lettuce

SERVES 6–8

Preheat the oven to 180°C (350°F/Gas 4). Remove the crusts from the bread and cut the bread into cubes. Place on a baking tray in a single layer and bake for 10 minutes, or until crisp and lightly golden. Cool completely.

Cut the feta into small cubes and put in a bowl. Combine the garlic, marjoram, chives, basil, vinegar and oil. Pour over the feta and cover with plastic wrap. Leave for at least 30 minutes, stirring occasionally. Wash and dry the lettuces. Tear the leaves into pieces and place in a bowl. Add the feta with dressing, the bread cubes and toss to combine.

PREPARATION TIME: 20 MINUTES +   COOKING TIME: 10 MINUTES

SPROUT AND PEAR SALAD WITH SESAME DRESSING

250 g (9 oz) snow pea (mangetout) sprouts
250 g (9 oz) bean sprouts
30 g (1 oz) chives
100 g (3¹/₂ oz) snow peas (mangetout)
1 celery stalk
2 firm pears (not green)
coriander (cilantro) sprigs
sesame seeds, to garnish

SESAME DRESSING
2 tablespoons soy sauce
1 teaspoon sesame oil
1 tablespoon soft brown sugar
2 tablespoons peanut oil
1 tablespoon rice vinegar

SERVES 6

Wash and drain the snow pea sprouts. Remove the brown tips from the bean sprouts.

Snip the chives into 4 cm (1¹/₂ inch) lengths and cut the snow peas and celery into thin matchstick strips.

Peel and core the pears then slice into thin strips, slightly wider than the celery and snow peas. Place in a bowl and cover with water to prevent discoloration.

To make the sesame dressing, combine the ingredients and mix thoroughly.

Drain the pears. Combine all the salad ingredients and the coriander sprigs in a large serving bowl. Pour the dressing over and toss lightly.

Sprinkle with sesame seeds and serve immediately.

PREPARATION TIME: 30 MINUTES   COOKING TIME: NIL

GREEN OLIVE, WALNUT AND POMEGRANATE SALAD

1 large red onion
100 g (3½ oz/1 cup) walnut halves
350 g (12 oz/2 cups) green olives, pitted and halved
175 g (6 oz/1 cup) pomegranate seeds
20 g (¾ oz) flat-leaf (Italian) parsley leaves

DRESSING
125 ml (4 fl oz/½ cup) olive oil
1½ tablespoons pomegranate syrup
½ teaspoon chilli flakes

SERVES 4

Chop the onion. Soak the walnut halves in boiling water for 3–4 minutes, or until the skins peel off readily. Drain, peel and pat dry. Lightly toast the walnuts under a medium grill (broiler) and when cool, roughly chop.

To make the dressing, combine all the ingredients and mix thoroughly.

Put the olives, pomegranate seeds, onion, walnuts and parsley in a bowl and toss. Just before serving, pour over the dressing, season to taste, and combine well.

PREPARATION TIME: 10 MINUTES   COOKING TIME: NIL

SPINACH AND NUT SALAD

250 g (9 oz) young green beans
30 English spinach leaves (about 90 g/3¼ oz)
½ onion
90 g (3¼ oz/⅓ cup) plain yoghurt
1 tablespoon lemon juice
1 tablespoon shredded mint
40 g (1½ oz/⅓ cup) chopped walnuts, toasted (see Note)
mint leaves, to serve
thin slices red capsicum (pepper), to serve

SERVES 4

Trim the beans then chop them. Rinse the spinach in cold water. Cover the beans with boiling water, leave for 2 minutes, then drain. Pat the spinach and beans dry with paper towel, then cool. Finely slice the onion.

Arrange the spinach, beans and onion on a serving plate. Mix the yoghurt, lemon juice and mint in a bowl. Pour over the salad, sprinkle with walnuts and garnish with mint leaves and slices of red capsicum.

PREPARATION TIME: 15 MINUTES   COOKING TIME: 2 MINUTES

NOTE: Toast the walnuts in a dry frying pan over medium heat, stirring constantly, until they are golden brown and fragrant. Watch carefully as they will burn easily.

Green olive, walnut and pomegranate salad

COOKED VEGETABLE SALAD

1 small turnip
1 large onion
2 celery stalks
200 g (7 oz) button mushrooms
1 large carrot
$1/2$ red capsicum (pepper)
4 spring onions (scallions)
2 tablespoons sesame oil
1 tablespoon oil
2 garlic cloves, finely chopped
80 g ($2^3/4$ oz/$1/2$ cup) pine nuts, toasted (see Note)

DRESSING
60 ml (2 fl oz/$1/4$ cup) soy sauce
1 tablespoon white vinegar
3 cm ($1^1/4$ inch) piece fresh ginger, very finely sliced and cut into fine strips
1–2 teaspoons soft brown sugar

SERVES 4

Cut the turnip into thin strips. Slice the onion into thin rings. Slice the celery stalks and the button mushrooms. Cut the carrot into fine strips. Cut the red capsicum in half, remove the seeds and membrane and cut into fine strips. Chop the spring onions.

Put the turnip on a plate lined with paper towel. Sprinkle with 2 teaspoons of salt and set aside for at least 20 minutes. Rinse the turnip under cold water and pat dry with paper towel.

Heat the combined oils in a large frying pan or wok and swirl to coat the base and side. Stir-fry the turnip, garlic and onion for 3 minutes over medium heat, or until lightly golden.

Add the celery, mushrooms, carrot, red capsicum and spring onion and toss well. Cover and steam for 1 minute. Remove the vegetables from the wok and set aside to cool.

To make the dressing, combine all the ingredients in a bowl. Pour the dressing over the cooled vegetables and toss. Arrange them on a serving plate and sprinkle with the pine nuts.

PREPARATION TIME: 45 MINUTES +   COOKING TIME: 15 MINUTES

NOTE: Toast the pine nuts in a dry frying pan over medium heat, stirring constantly, until they are golden brown and fragrant. Watch carefully as they will burn easily.

CHICKPEA AND OLIVE SALAD

330 g (11³/4 oz/1¹/2 cups) dried chickpeas
1 small Lebanese (short) cucumber
2 tomatoes
1 small red onion
3 tablespoons chopped flat-leaf (Italian) parsley
60 g (2¹/4 oz/¹/2 cup) pitted black olives

DRESSING
1 tablespoon lemon juice
60 ml (2 fl oz/¹/4 cup) olive oil
1 garlic clove, crushed
1 teaspoon honey

SERVES 6

Place the chickpeas in a large bowl and cover with cold water. Leave to soak overnight.

Drain the chickpeas, place in a saucepan, cover with fresh water and cook for 25 minutes, or until just tender. Drain and leave to cool.

Cut the cucumber in half lengthways, scoop out the seeds and cut into 1 cm (¹/2 inch) slices. Cut the tomatoes into cubes roughly the same size as the chickpeas, and finely chop the onion.

Combine the chickpeas, cucumber, tomato, onion, parsley and olives in a serving bowl.

To make the dressing, combine all the ingredients. Pour over the salad and toss lightly to combine. Serve at room temperature.

PREPARATION TIME: 20 MINUTES +   COOKING TIME: 25 MINUTES

AVOCADO SALSA

1 red onion
2 large avocados
1 tablespoon lime juice
1 tomato
1 small red capsicum (pepper)
1 teaspoon ground coriander
1 teaspoon ground cumin
3 tablespoons chopped coriander (cilantro) leaves
2 tablespoons olive oil
4-5 drops Tabasco sauce

SERVES 6

Finely chop the onion. Cut the avocados in half, remove the stones and carefully peel. Finely chop the flesh. Put the flesh in a bowl and toss lightly with the lime juice.

Cut the tomato in half horizontally, squeeze gently to remove the seeds and finely chop. Cut the capsicum in half, remove the seeds and membrane and finely chop.

Put the ground coriander and cumin in a small frying pan and stir over medium heat for 1 minute to enhance the fragrance and flavour. Cool. Add all the ingredients to the avocado and gently combine, so that the avocado retains its shape and is not mashed. Refrigerate until required. Serve at room temperature with corn chips.

PREPARATION TIME: 15 MINUTES   COOKING TIME: 1 MINUTE

Chickpea and olive salad

GRILLED VEGETABLE SALAD

1 red onion
6 small eggplants (aubergines), about 16 cm
(6$\frac{1}{4}$ inches) long (not pencil eggplant)
4 red capsicums (peppers)
4 orange capsicums (peppers)
1 tablespoon baby capers
80 ml (2$\frac{1}{2}$ fl oz/$\frac{1}{3}$ cup) good-quality
olive oil
1 tablespoon chopped flat-leaf (Italian)
parsley
2 garlic cloves, finely chopped

SERVES 4

Without slicing through the base, cut the onion from top to base into six sections, leaving it attached at the base.

Put the onion on a barbecue, or over an open-flamed grill or gas stovetop, with the eggplants and capsicums. Cook the vegetables over moderate heat for about 10 minutes, turning them occasionally, until the eggplants and capsicum skins are blackened and blistered. Cool the capsicums in a plastic bag for 10 minutes and set the onion and eggplant aside.

Dry-fry the capers with a pinch of salt until crisp. Cut the onion into its six sections and discard the charred outer skins.

Peel the skins off the eggplants and remove the stalk. Cut from top to bottom into slices. Peel the capsicums, cut them in half and remove the seeds and membrane. Cut into wide slices.

Arrange all the vegetables on a large serving platter. Drizzle the olive oil over them and season. Scatter the parsley, garlic and capers over the top. Serve cold.

PREPARATION TIME: 15 MINUTES +   COOKING TIME: 10 MINUTES

NOTE: Grilling the vegetables under a griller (broiler) or roasting them in a hot oven also works, although the dish will lack the characteristic smoky flavour.

ORANGE AND DATE SALAD

6 navel oranges
2 teaspoons orange blossom water
8 dates, stoned and thinly sliced, lengthways
90 g (3¼ oz/¾ cup) slivered almonds, lightly toasted (see Notes)
1 tablespoon shredded mint
¼ teaspoon ras el hanout (see Notes) or cinnamon

SERVES 4–6

Peel all the oranges, removing all the pith. Section them by cutting away all the membrane from the flesh. Place the segments in a bowl and squeeze the juice from the remainder of the oranges over them. Add the orange blossom water and stir gently to combine. Cover with plastic wrap and refrigerate until chilled.

Place the orange segments and the juice on a large flat serving dish and scatter the dates and almonds over the top. Sprinkle the mint and ras el hanout over the orange segments. Serve chilled.

PREPARATION TIME: 30 MINUTES +   COOKING TIME: NIL

NOTES: Toast the almonds in a dry frying pan over medium heat, stirring constantly, until they are lightly golden. Watch carefully as they will burn easily.

Ras el hanout is a spice mixture commonly used in Moroccan cooking.

SPINACH AND AVOCADO SALAD WITH WARM MUSTARD VINAIGRETTE

30 English spinach leaves (about 90 g/3¼ oz)
1 red or green curly-leafed lettuce
2 avocados
60 ml (2 fl oz/¼ cup) olive oil
2 teaspoons sesame seeds
1 tablespoon lemon juice
2 teaspoons wholegrain mustard

SERVES 8

Wash and thoroughly dry the spinach and lettuce leaves. Tear the leaves into bite-sized pieces and place in a large serving bowl.

Peel the avocados and cut the flesh into thin slices. Scatter over the leaves. Heat 1 tablespoon of the oil in a small frying pan. Add the sesame seeds and cook over low heat until they just start to turn golden. Remove from the heat immediately and allow to cool slightly.

Add the lemon juice, remaining oil and mustard to the pan and stir to combine. While still warm, pour over the salad and toss gently to coat the leaves. This salad is best served immediately.

PREPARATION TIME: 15 MINUTES   COOKING TIME: 2 MINUTES

Orange and date salad

MEDITERRANEAN LENTIL SALAD

1 large red capsicum (pepper)
1 large yellow capsicum (pepper)
250 g (9 oz/1 cup) red lentils
1 red onion, finely chopped
1 Lebanese (short) cucumber, chopped

DRESSING
80 ml (2½ fl oz/⅓ cup) olive oil
2 tablespoons lemon juice
1 teaspoon ground cumin
2 garlic cloves, crushed

SERVES 4–6

Cut the capsicums in half lengthways. Remove the seeds and membrane and then cut them into large, flattish pieces. Grill (broil) the capsicum until the skin blackens and blisters.

Put the capsicum on a cutting board, cover with a tea towel (dish towel) and leave to cool. Peel the capsicum and cut the flesh into 5 mm (¼ inch) strips.

Cook the lentils in boiling water for 10 minutes, or until tender (do not overcook, as they will become mushy). Drain well. Put the capsicum, lentils, onion and cucumber in a bowl and toss to combine.

To make the dressing, put the olive oil, lemon juice, cumin, garlic and some salt and pepper into a small bowl and whisk to combine.

Pour the dressing over the salad and mix well. Cover the salad and refrigerate for 4 hours.

Allow the salad to return to room temperature before serving.

PREPARATION TIME: 20 MINUTES +   COOKING TIME: 20 MINUTES

TOFU SALAD

2 teaspoons Thai sweet chilli sauce
1/2 teaspoon grated fresh ginger
1 garlic clove, crushed
2 teaspoons soy sauce
2 tablespoons oil
250 g (9 oz) firm tofu
100 g (3½ oz) snow peas (mangetout)
2 small carrots
100 g (3½ oz) red cabbage
2 tablespoons chopped peanuts

SERVES 4

Combine the chilli sauce, ginger, garlic, soy sauce and oil. Cut the tofu into 2 cm (³/4 inch) cubes. Place the tofu in a bowl, pour the marinade over and stir. Cover with plastic wrap and refrigerate for 1 hour.

Slice the snow peas into 3 cm (1¹/4 inch lengths). Put them in a small saucepan, pour boiling water over and leave to stand for 1 minute, then drain and transfer to iced water. Drain well. Cut the carrots into batons and finely shred the cabbage.

Add the snow peas, carrots and cabbage to the tofu and toss lightly to combine. Transfer to a serving bowl or individual plates, sprinkle with peanuts and serve immediately.

PREPARATION TIME: 20 MINUTES +   COOKING TIME: NIL

CURLY ENDIVE AND BLUE CHEESE SALAD

3 slices bread
60 ml (2 fl oz/¹/4 cup) oil
30 g (1 oz) butter
1 curly endive
125 g (4½ oz) blue cheese
2 tablespoons olive oil
3 teaspoons white wine vinegar
2 tablespoons snipped chives

SERVES 6

To make the croutons, remove the crusts from the bread, discarding the crusts. Cut the bread into small squares.

Heat the oil and butter in a frying pan until bubbling and add the bread. Cook, tossing frequently, for 3 minutes or until golden. Drain on paper towel.

Wash and dry the endive thoroughly. Place the leaves in a serving bowl and crumble the blue cheese over the top.

Combine the oil and vinegar. Drizzle over the salad, add the chives and croutons and toss. Serve immediately.

PREPARATION TIME: 15 MINUTES   COOKING TIME: 5 MINUTES

SNOW PEA SALAD

200 g (7 oz) snow peas (mangetout)
1 large red capsicum (pepper)
4 leaves oak leaf lettuce
5 leaves green coral lettuce
250 g (9 oz) cherry tomatoes
60 g (2¼ oz) watercress sprigs
parmesan cheese shavings, to serve
(see Note)

GARLIC CROUTONS
3 slices white bread
60 ml (2 fl oz/¼ cup) olive oil
1 garlic clove, crushed

DRESSING
2 tablespoons olive oil
1 tablespoon mayonnaise
1 tablespoon sour cream
2 tablespoons lemon juice
1 teaspoon soft brown sugar

SERVES 4–6

Slice the snow peas diagonally. Cut the red capsicum in half, remove the seeds and membrane and slice.

Combine the snow peas, red capsicum, lettuces, tomatoes and watercress in a large bowl.

To make the croutons, remove the crusts from the bread and discard the crusts. Cut the bread into 1 cm (½ inch) squares. Heat the olive oil in a small, heavy-based frying pan and add the crushed garlic. Stir in the bread cubes and cook until golden and crisp. Remove from the heat and leave to drain well on paper towel.

To make the dressing, whisk all the ingredients together with some cracked black pepper in a small bowl for 2 minutes, or until combined.

Just before serving, top with the croutons and parmesan shavings then pour the dressing over the salad, stirring until well combined.

PREPARATION TIME: 25 MINUTES   COOKING TIME: 5 MINUTES

NOTE: Use a vegetable peeler to make thin shavings of parmesan.

SWEET AND SOUR ONIONS

3 red onions (about 500 g/1 lb 2 oz)
2 tablespoons wholegrain mustard
2 tablespoons honey
2 tablespoons red wine vinegar
2 tablespoons oil

SERVES 4–6

Preheat the oven to 220°C (425°F/Gas 7).

Carefully peel the onions, keeping the ends intact so that the layers stay together. Cut the onions into eight pieces and put the pieces in a non-stick ovenproof dish.

Combine the mustard, honey, red wine vinegar and oil. Brush this mixture over the onions, cover the dish and bake for 20 minutes. Uncover and continue baking for another 15–20 minutes, or until the onions are soft and caramelized.

PREPARATION TIME: 10 MINUTES   COOKING TIME 40 MINUTES

KOREAN PICKLED BEAN SPROUTS

300 g (10½ oz) bean sprouts, trimmed
2 tablespoons soy sauce
2 tablespoons rice vinegar
1½ teaspoons sesame oil
½ teaspoon sugar
20 g (¾ oz/⅓ cup) thinly sliced spring onions (scallions)
1 tablespoon toasted sesame seeds (see Notes)

SERVES 4

Blanch the bean sprouts in a saucepan of boiling water for 1–2 minutes, or until softened but still a little crunchy. Drain, rinse under cold water and drain again.

Combine the remaining ingredients with a pinch of salt and a little finely ground black pepper, then pour over the bean sprouts and mix. Chill for 2 hours before serving.

PREPARATION TIME: 10 MINUTES +   COOKING TIME: NIL

NOTES: Toast the sesame seeds in a dry frying pan over medium heat, stirring constantly, until they are lightly golden and fragrant. Watch carefully as they will burn easily.

You can also mix ½ teaspoon chilli flakes in the marinade if you like things a little spicy.

PUMPKIN WITH CHILLI AND AVOCADO

750 g (1 lb 10 oz) pumpkin (winter squash)
1 large avocado

DRESSING
1 small red onion
2 tablespoons olive oil
1 tablespoon chopped coriander
(cilantro) leaves
1 tablespoon chopped mint
2 teaspoons sweet chilli sauce
2 teaspoons balsamic vinegar
1 teaspoon soft brown sugar

SERVES 6

Scrape the seeds from the inside of the pumpkin. Cut the pumpkin into slices and remove the skin. Cook in a large saucepan of simmering water until tender but still firm. Remove from the heat and drain well.

To make the dressing, finely chop the red onion. Combine the onion with the remaining ingredients in a small bowl.

Cut the avocado in half. Remove the stone using a sharp-bladed knife. Peel and discard the skin from the avocado, then cut the flesh in thin slices.

Combine the warm pumpkin and avocado in a serving bowl. Gently toss the coriander dressing through. Serve immediately.

PREPARATION TIME: 20 MINUTES   COOKING TIME: 10 MINUTES

NOTES: Assemble this dish just before serving. The dressing can be made up several hours in advance. Store, covered, in the refrigerator.

Add one small red chilli, finely chopped, to the dressing if you want a spicier flavour.

OKRA WITH CORIANDER AND TOMATO SAUCE

1 onion
60 ml (2 fl oz/¼ cup) olive oil
2 garlic cloves, crushed
500 g (1 lb 2 oz) fresh okra (see Note)
400 g (14 oz) tinned chopped good quality tomatoes
2 teaspoons sugar
60 ml (2 fl oz/¼ cup) lemon juice
60 g (2¼ oz) coriander (cilantro), finely chopped

SERVES 4–6

Chop the onion. Heat the oil in a large frying pan, add the onion and cook over medium heat for 5 minutes, or until transparent and golden. Add the garlic and cook for another minute.

Add the okra to the pan and cook, stirring, for 4–5 minutes, then add the tomato, sugar and lemon juice and simmer, stirring occasionally, for 3–4 minutes, or until softened.

Stir in the coriander, remove from the heat and serve.

PREPARATION TIME: 5 MINUTES   COOKING TIME: 15 MINUTES

NOTE: If fresh okra is not available, you can use 800 g (1 lb 12 oz) of tinned okra instead. Rinse and drain the okra before adding with the coriander.

BRAISED ARTICHOKES WITH BROAD BEANS

1 lemon
6 large globe artichokes
4 spring onions (scallions)
80 ml (2½ fl oz/⅓ cup) extra virgin olive oil
300 g (10½ oz) shelled broad (fava) beans
3 tablespoons chopped dill

SERVES 4

Squeeze the lemon into a large bowl of water and put the skin shells in the water to make acidulated water. Using a small sharp knife, remove the choke from each artichoke and peel away the prickly outer leaves. Trim the bases.

Cut each artichoke into quarters and put them in the acidulated water, to prevent them browning, while you prepare the rest. Thinly slice the spring onions.

In a large heavy-based, non-aluminium saucepan, heat the oil and cook the spring onion for 1–2 minutes, or until just softened. Add the drained artichokes, beans and dill and add just enough water to cover the vegetables. Cover and simmer for 30 minutes, or until tender. Drain the excess water and season. Serve warm, or at room temperature.

PREPARATION TIME: 25 MINUTES   COOKING TIME: 35 MINUTES

Okra with coriander and tomato sauce

RATATOUILLE

6 vine-ripened tomatoes
500 g (1 lb 2 oz) eggplants (aubergines)
375 g (13 oz) zucchini (courgettes)
1 green capsicum (pepper)
1 red onion
100 ml (3½ fl oz) olive oil
3 garlic cloves, finely chopped
¼ teaspoon cayenne pepper
2 teaspoons chopped thyme
2 bay leaves
1 tablespoon red wine vinegar
1 teaspoon caster (superfine) sugar
3 tablespoons shredded basil

SERVES 4–6

Score a cross in the base of each tomato. Put in a heatproof bowl and cover with boiling water. Leave for 30 seconds, then transfer to cold water, drain and peel away the skin from the cross. Cut the tomatoes in half, scoop out the seeds and chop the flesh.

Cut the eggplants and zucchini into 2 cm (¾ inch) cubes. Cut the green capsicum in half, remove the seeds and membrane and cut into 2 cm (¾ inch) squares. Cut the red onion into 2 cm (¾ inch) wedges.

Heat 2 tablespoons of the oil in a large saucepan, add the eggplant and cook over medium heat for 4–5 minutes, or until softened but not browned. Remove the eggplant from the pan. Add another 2 tablespoons oil to the pan, add the zucchini and cook for 3–4 minutes, or until softened. Remove. Add the green capsicum, cook for 2 minutes and remove.

Heat the remaining oil, add the onion and cook for 2–3 minutes, or until softened. Add the garlic, cayenne pepper, thyme and bay leaves and cook, stirring, for 1 minute.

Return the eggplant, zucchini and capsicum to the pan and add the tomato, vinegar and sugar. Simmer for 20 minutes, stirring occasionally. Stir in the basil and season. Serve hot or at room temperature.

PREPARATION TIME: 25 MINUTES   COOKING TIME: 40 MINUTES

NOTE: You can also serve ratatouille as a starter with bread.

ALGERIAN EGGPLANT JAM

2 eggplants (aubergines) (about 400 g/14 oz)
olive oil, for pan-frying
2 garlic cloves, crushed
1 teaspoon sweet paprika
1½ teaspoons ground cumin
½ teaspoon sugar
1 tablespoon lemon juice

SERVES 6–8

Cut the eggplant into 1 cm (½ inch) slices. Sprinkle with some salt and drain in a colander for 30 minutes. Rinse well, squeeze gently and pat dry.

Heat 5 mm (¼ inch) of oil in a large frying pan and fry the eggplant in batches over medium heat until golden brown on both sides. Drain on paper towel, then chop finely. Put in a colander until most of the oil has drained off then transfer to a bowl and add the garlic, paprika, cumin and sugar.

Wipe out the pan, add the eggplant mixture and stir constantly over medium heat for 2 minutes. Transfer to a bowl, stir in the lemon juice and season. Serve at room temperature.

PREPARATION TIME: 10 MINUTES +   COOKING TIME: 20 MINUTES

POTATO AND OIL PURÉE

1 kg (2 lb 4 oz) roasting potatoes
200 ml (7 fl oz) vegetable stock
2 garlic cloves, bruised
2 thyme sprigs
150 ml (5 fl oz) extra-virgin olive oil

SERVES 4

Cut the potatoes into large chunks and cook in a saucepan of boiling salted water until tender but still firm. While the potatoes are cooking, heat the stock in a small saucepan with the garlic and thyme. Bring to simmering point then remove from the heat and leave to infuse.

Drain the potatoes well and pass them through a mouli or mash them with a potato masher. Strain the stock, return to the saucepan, add the olive oil and reheat gently. Place the potato purée in a bowl and add the stock in a thin steady stream, stirring continuously with a flat wooden spoon. Season then beat well until the purée is smooth.

PREPARATION TIME: 5 MINUTES   COOKING TIME: 20 MINUTES

Algerian eggplant jam

SWEET GARLIC EGGPLANT

3 eggplants (aubergines)
145 ml (4³/₄ fl oz) oil
1¹/₂ teaspoons finely chopped garlic
2 tablespoons caster (superfine) sugar
30 ml (1 fl oz) soy sauce
30 ml (1 fl oz) cider vinegar
1 tablespoon dry sherry

SERVES 4

Cut the eggplants in half lengthways and then slice into wedges about 3 cm (1¹/₄ inches) wide. Cut the wedges into pieces about 3 cm (1¹/₄ inches) long.

Heat 60 ml (2 fl oz/¹/₄ cup) of the oil in a wok or heavy-based frying pan, swirling gently to coat the base and side. Add half the eggplant and stir-fry over high heat for 5 minutes, or until browned and all the oil has been absorbed. Transfer to a plate. Repeat the cooking procedure with another 60 ml (2 fl oz/¹/₄ cup) oil and the remaining eggplant.

Heat the remaining oil in the wok, swirling gently to coat the base and side. Add the garlic and cook slowly until just golden. Add the sugar, soy sauce, vinegar and sherry. Bring to the boil, stirring. Add the eggplant and simmer for 3 minutes to allow it to absorb the sauce. Serve at room temperature.

PREPARATION TIME: 5 MINUTES   COOKING TIME: 15 MINUTES

NOTE: This dish can be cooked up to 2 days ahead and refrigerated until required.

SAUTÉED ROSEMARY POTATOES

750 g (1 lb 10 oz) small new potatoes, unpeeled
30 g (1 oz) butter
2 tablespoons olive oil
2 garlic cloves, crushed
1 tablespoon finely chopped rosemary
1 teaspoon coarse rock rock or sea salt

SERVES 4–6

Wash the potatoes, pat dry with paper towel, then cut them in half. Lightly boil or steam the potatoes until they are just tender. Drain and cool slightly.

Heat the butter and oil in a large heavy-based frying pan. When the mixture is foaming, add the potatoes and season with pepper. Cook over medium heat for 5–10 minutes, or until golden and crisp, tossing regularly to ensure that the potatoes are evenly coloured.

Stir in the garlic, rosemary and salt. Cook for 1 minute or until well coated. Add $\frac{1}{2}$ teaspoon cracked black pepper and mix well. Serve hot or warm.

PREPARATION TIME: 15–20 MINUTES   COOKING TIME: 35 MINUTES

SPICED CORN

425 g (15 oz) tinned baby corn, drained
1 tablespoon oil
1 garlic clove, crushed
1 teaspoon chopped red chilli
$\frac{1}{2}$ teaspoon ground cumin

SERVES 2–4

Pat dry the baby corn with paper towel.

Heat the oil in a wok and swirl to coat the base and side. Add the garlic, chilli and ground cumin and stir-fry for 30 seconds. Add the corn and stir-fry for 3 minutes, or until heated through. Serve immediately.

PREPARATION TIME: 5 MINUTES   COOKING TIME: 5 MINUTES

NOTE: Spicy corn is so quick to make, it is an excellent last-minute accompaniment to a meal where a little zest is needed.

Sautéed rosemary potatoes

SPRING ONION AND CELERY BUNDLES

4 celery stalks
24 spring onions (scallions)
30 g (1 oz) butter
1 teaspoon celery seeds
1 tablespoon honey
125 ml (4 fl oz/½ cup) vegetable stock
1 teaspoon soy sauce
1 teaspoon cornflour (cornstarch) blended
with 1 teaspoon water

SERVES 6

Cut the celery into 10 cm (4 inch) lengths, then into strips the same thickness as the spring onions. Cut the root from the spring onions. Cut the spring onions into 10 cm (4 inch) lengths. Reserve the spring onion tops for ties. Plunge the spring onion tops into boiling water for 30 seconds, or until they are bright green, then transfer immediately into iced water. Drain and pat dry with paper towel.

Combine the spring onion and celery strips. Divide evenly into six bundles. Tie each bundle firmly with a spring onion top.

Heat the butter in a frying pan. Fry the bundles quickly over medium-high heat for 1 minute on each side. Remove from the pan. Add the celery seeds and cook for 30 seconds. Add the honey, stock, soy sauce, and blended cornflour and water. Bring to the boil, then reduce the heat, stirring continuously. Add the spring onion and celery bundles. Simmer gently for 7 minutes, or until the bundles are just tender. Serve immediately with the cooking liquid.

PREPARATION TIME: 20 MINUTES   COOKING TIME: 10 MINUTES

GREEN BEANS IN SESAME SEED SAUCE

500 g (1 lb 2 oz) slender green beans, trimmed
2 tablespoons Japanese white sesame seeds (see Notes)
6 cm (2¹/₂ inch) piece fresh ginger
1 tablespoon Japanese soy sauce
1 tablespoon mirin
3 teaspoons sugar
1 teaspoon Japanese white sesame seeds, extra

SERVES 4

Cook the beans in a large saucepan of boiling water for 2 minutes. Drain, then plunge into iced water to stop the cooking process. Drain again and set aside.

Toast the sesame seeds in a dry frying pan, over medium heat, for about 5 minutes shaking the pan constantly until the seeds are golden brown. Pound the seeds using a mortar and pestle until a paste is formed (the mixture will become damp as oil is released from the seeds).

Combine the sesame seed paste with the ginger, soy sauce, mirin and sugar. Pour the sauce over the beans, scatter over the extra sesame seeds and serve.

PREPARATION TIME: 10 MINUTES   COOKING TIME: 10 MINUTES

NOTES: The beans can be marinated in the sauce overnight.
Japanese sesame seeds are plump and large, with a fuller flavour than other sesame seeds.

SPICY EGGPLANT SLICES

2 eggplants (aubergines)
salt, to sprinkle
40 g (1¹/₂ oz/¹/₃ cup) plain (all-purpose) flour
2 teaspoons ground cumin
2 teaspoons ground coriander
1 teaspoon chilli powder
oil, for pan-frying
125 g (4¹/₂ oz/¹/₂ cup) plain yoghurt
1 tablespoon chopped mint

SERVES 4–6

Cut the eggplants into 1 cm (¹/₂ inch) slices. Arrange in a single layer on a tray and cover well with salt. Leave for 15 minutes, then rinse and pat dry thoroughly with paper towel.

Sift the flour and spices onto a plate. Dust the eggplant slices with the flour mixture, shaking off any excess. Heat about 2 cm (³/₄ inch) of oil in a heavy-based frying pan. Cook the eggplant slices a few at a time, for 2–3 minutes each side, or until golden. Drain on paper towel. Combine the yoghurt and mint. Serve with the warm eggplant.

PREPARATION TIME: 15 MINUTES +   COOKING TIME: 15 MINUTES

Green beans in sesame seed sauce

ANDALUSIAN ASPARAGUS

500 g (1 lb 2 oz) asparagus
1 thick slice crusty country bread
60 ml (2 fl oz/¼ cup) extra virgin olive oil
2–3 garlic cloves
12 blanched almonds
1 teaspoon paprika
1 teaspoon ground cumin
1 tablespoon red wine or sherry vinegar

SERVES 4

Trim the woody ends from the asparagus. Remove and discard the crusts from the bread and cut the bread into cubes.

Heat the oil in a heavy-based frying pan and cook the bread, garlic and almonds over medium heat for 2–3 minutes, or until all the ingredients are golden. Using a slotted spoon, transfer to a food processor and add the paprika, cumin, vinegar, some salt and pepper and 1 tablespoon water. Process until the mixture forms a coarse meal.

Return the frying pan to the heat and add the asparagus with a little extra oil if necessary. Cook over medium heat for 3–5 minutes, then add the bread and almond mixture with 200 ml (7 fl oz) water. Simmer for 3–4 minutes, or until the asparagus is tender but still firm to the bite and most of the liquid has boiled away. Serve.

PREPARATION TIME: 10 MINUTES   COOKING TIME: 15 MINUTES

LEEKS IN WHITE SAUCE

2 leeks, white part only
50 g (1³/₄ oz) butter
1 tablespoon plain (all-purpose) flour
250 ml (9 fl oz/1 cup) milk
2 tablespoons grated cheddar cheese
1 tablespoon dry breadcrumbs

SERVES 6

Wash the leek well, cut in half lengthways and then into 5 cm (2 inch) pieces. Heat 30 g (1 oz) of the butter in a heavy-based saucepan, add the leeks and cook for 10 minutes, stirring, until tender. Transfer to an ovenproof serving dish.

Melt the remaining butter in a frying pan over low heat. Stir in the flour and cook for 1 minute, or until pale and foaming. Remove from the heat and gradually stir in the milk. Return to the heat and stir until the sauce boils and thickens. Pour over the leeks. Sprinkle with cheese and breadcrumbs. Grill (broil) for 2–3 minutes, or until golden brown.

PREPARATION TIME: 15 MINUTES   COOKING TIME: 15 MINUTES

CANDIED PUMPKIN

500 g (1 lb 2 oz) pumpkin (winter squash)
30 g (1 oz) butter
2 tablespoons pouring (whipping) cream
1 tablespoon soft brown sugar
snipped chives, to garnish

SERVES 4

Preheat the oven to 180°C (350°F/Gas 4). Remove the membrane and seeds from the pumpkin and cut the flesh into thin slices. Place the slices, overlapping, in a 1 litre (32 fl oz/4 cup) ovenproof dish.

Put the butter, cream and sugar in a small saucepan over low heat. Stir until smooth, then pour the mixture over the pumpkin. Bake for 35 minutes, or until the pumpkin is tender. Sprinkle with the chives before serving.

PREPARATION TIME: 20 MINUTES   COOKING TIME: 40 MINUTES

SWEET POTATO ROSTI

3 orange sweet potatoes, unpeeled
2 teaspoons cornflour (cornstarch)
40 g (1½ oz) butter
150 g (5½ oz) mozzarella cheese, cut into
30 cubes

MAKES 30

Boil or microwave the sweet potatoes until almost cooked, but still firm. Set aside to cool, then peel and roughly grate into a bowl. Add the cornflour and ½ teaspoon salt and toss lightly to combine.

Melt a little of the butter in a frying pan. Place teaspoons of the potato in the pan and put a cube of cheese in the centre of each mound. Top with another teaspoon of potato and gently flatten to form rough circles. Increase the heat to medium and cook for about 3 minutes each side, or until golden. Repeat with remaining potato mixture and mozzarella cubes.

PREPARATION TIME: 30 MINUTES   COOKING TIME: 45 MINUTES

NOTE: The sweet potato can be cooked and grated up to 2 hours ahead and set aside, covered, until serving time. Assemble and cook the rosti close to serving time.

SPINACH WITH RAISINS AND PINE NUTS

500 g (1 lb 2 oz) English spinach
1 small red onion
2 tablespoons pine nuts
1 tablespoon olive oil
1 garlic clove, thinly sliced
2 tablespoons raisins
pinch ground cinnamon

SERVES 6

Trim the stalks from the spinach and discard. Wash and shred the leaves. Slice the onion.

Put the pine nuts in a frying pan and stir over medium heat for 3 minutes, or until lightly brown. Remove from the pan.

Heat the oil in the pan, add the onion and cook over low heat, stirring occasionally, for 10 minutes, or until translucent. Increase the heat to medium, add the garlic and cook for 1 minute. Add the spinach with the water clinging to it, the raisins and cinnamon. Cover and cook for 2 minutes, or until the spinach wilts. Stir in the pine nuts, and season to taste.

PREPARATION TIME: 15 MINUTES   COOKING TIME: 15 MINUTES

NOTE: Silverbeet (Swiss chard) works equally well in this recipe, although it may take a little longer to cook than spinach.

BEANS WITH TOMATOES

500 g (1 lb 2 oz) green beans
440 g (15^1/$_2$ oz) tinned tomatoes
1 large onion
2 tablespoons olive oil
1 garlic clove, crushed
2 teaspoons sugar
2 tablespoons red wine vinegar
1 tablespoon chopped basil
3 tablespoons chopped olives (optional)
basil leaves, to garnish

SERVES 6

Trim the tops and tails from the beans and cut the beans in half. Cook in boiling water for 3 minutes, drain, then rinse in cold water to refresh the colour. Set aside. Chop the tomatoes, reserving the juice. Chop the onion.

Heat the oil in a frying pan. Add the onion and garlic and cook, stirring, until the onion starts to brown. Sprinkle the sugar over the onion and cook until it caramelizes. Add the vinegar and cook for 1 minute. Add the tomatoes and juice, basil, olives and some pepper. Simmer, uncovered, for 5 minutes.

Add the beans and simmer until warmed through. Serve garnished with basil leaves.

PREPARATION TIME: 15 MINUTES   COOKING TIME: 20 MINUTES

BAKED ROOT VEGETABLES WITH SWEET GINGER GLAZE

150 g (5½ oz) orange sweet potato
1 potato
1 carrot
1 parsnip
1 turnip
2 tablespoons olive oil
60 g (2¼ oz) butter
2 tablespoons caster (superfine) sugar
1 tablespoon finely grated fresh ginger

SERVES 4–6

Preheat the oven to 210°C (415°F/Gas 6-7). Brush a large baking tray with oil.

Cut the sweet potato, potato, carrot, parsnip and turnip into sticks about 5 cm (2 inches) long and 1 cm (½ inch) thick.

Place the vegetables in a single layer on the prepared baking tray and brush them all over with olive oil. Bake for 1 hour, or until golden.

Melt the butter in a small saucepan. Add the sugar and stir over low heat until the sugar has dissolved. Add the grated ginger and 60 ml (2 fl oz/¼ cup) water and stir to combine. Bring to the boil, reduce the heat to low and simmer, uncovered, for 5 minutes, or until the mixture has reduced and thickened slightly. Pour the glaze over the baked vegetables, toss to coat and return the tray to the oven for 5 minutes. Serve immediately.

PREPARATION TIME: 25 MINUTES   COOKING TIME: 1 HOUR 10 MINUTES

PASTA, NOODLES AND RICE

SPICED CARROT AND FETA GNOCCHI

1 kg (2 lb 4 oz) carrots
200 g (7 oz) feta cheese, crumbled
280 g (10 oz/2¼ cups) plain (all-purpose) flour
¼ teaspoon ground nutmeg
¼ teaspoon garam masala
1 egg, lightly beaten

MINTED CREAM SAUCE
2 spring onions (scallions)
30 g (1 oz) butter
2 garlic cloves, crushed
250 ml (9 fl oz/1 cup) pouring (whipping) cream
2 tablespoons shredded mint

SERVES 6–8

Cut the carrots into large pieces and steam, boil or microwave until tender. Drain and allow to cool slightly before transferring to a food processor.

Process the carrot and the feta together until smooth. Transfer the mixture to a large bowl. Stir in the sifted flour, spices and egg, and mix to form a soft dough.

Lightly coat your fingertips with flour and shape teaspoons of the mixture into flat circles.

To make the minted cream sauce, slice the spring onion. Melt the butter in a frying pan, add the garlic and spring onion and cook over medium heat for 3 minutes, or until the garlic is soft and golden. Add the cream, bring to the boil then reduce the heat and simmer for 3 minutes, or until the cream has thickened slightly. Remove from the heat and stir through the mint.

Meanwhile, cook the gnocchi, in batches, in a large saucepan of boiling salted water for about 2 minutes, or until they float to the surface. Use a slotted spoon to transfer to warmed serving plates. Drizzle the minted cream sauce over the gnocchi and serve.

PREPARATION TIME: 45 MINUTES   COOKING TIME: 40 MINUTES

NOTE: This mixture is not as firm as some other gnocchi recipes. Make sure the dough is put on a lightly floured surface and keep your fingertips coated in flour when you are shaping the gnocchi.

TOFU, PEANUT AND NOODLE STIR-FRY

1 red capsicum (pepper)
250 g (9 oz) firm tofu
1 onion
125 g (4^1/$_2$ oz) broccoli
2 garlic cloves, crushed
1 teaspoon grated fresh ginger
80 ml (2^1/$_2$ fl oz/^{1}/$_3$ cup) kecap manis (see Note)
90 g (3^1/$_4$ oz/^{1}/$_3$ cup) peanut butter
2 tablespoons peanut or vegetable oil
500 g (1 lb 2 oz) hokkien (egg) noodles

SERVES 4

Cut the capsicum in half, remove the seeds and membrane and chop. Cut the tofu into 1.5 cm (5/8 inch) cubes. Chop the onion and cut the broccoli into small florets. Combine the tofu with the garlic, ginger and half the kecap manis in a small bowl. Put the peanut butter, 125 ml (4 fl oz/^{1}/$_2$ cup) water and remaining kecap manis in another bowl and mix.

Heat a wok over high heat, add the oil and swirl to coat the base and side. Drain the tofu and reserve the marinade. Cook the tofu in two batches in the hot oil until well browned. Remove from the wok.

Put the noodles in a large heatproof bowl. Cover with boiling water and leave for 1 minute. Drain and gently separate the noodles. Add the vegetables to the wok (add a little more oil if necessary) and stir-fry until just tender. Add the tofu, reserved marinade and noodles to the wok. Add the peanut butter mixture and toss until heated through.

PREPARATION TIME: 15 MINUTES   COOKING TIME: 5 MINUTES

NOTE: Kecap manis is an Indonesian sweet soy sauce. If you are unable to find it, use soy sauce sweetened with a little soft brown sugar.

SPAGHETTI WITH HERBS AND TOMATO

20 g (3/4 oz/^{1}/$_4$ cup) fresh breadcrumbs
500 g (1 lb 2 oz) spaghetti
60 ml (2 fl oz/^{1}/$_4$ cup) olive oil
2 garlic cloves, diced
30 g (1 oz) chopped herbs (such as basil, coriander, parsley)
4 tomatoes, chopped
30 g (1 oz/^{1}/$_4$ cup) chopped walnuts
25 g (1 oz/^{1}/$_4$ cup) grated parmesan cheese, plus extra, to serve

SERVES 4

Heat the grill (broiler) to medium and put the fresh breadcrumbs under for a few seconds, or until slightly golden.

Cook the spaghetti in a saucepan of rapidly boiling salted water until *al dente*, then drain.

Heat 2 tablespoons of the olive oil in a large frying pan and cook the garlic until soft. Add the remaining oil and the herbs, tomato, walnuts and parmesan. Add the cooked pasta to the pan and toss for 1–2 minutes. Top with the breadcrumbs and extra parmesan.

PREPARATION TIME: 20 MINUTES   COOKING TIME: 15 MINUTES

Tofu, peanut and noodle stir-fry

WILD RICE, THYME AND MIXED MUSHROOM PILAFF

125 g (4¹/₂ oz/²/₃ cup) wild rice
375 ml (13 fl oz/1¹/₂ cups) vegetable stock
1 large onion
300 g (10¹/₂ oz) mixed mushrooms
(such as button, field, Swiss brown)
60 g (2¹/₄ oz) butter
2 garlic cloves, crushed
265 g (9¹/₂ oz/1¹/₃ cups) long-grain white rice
1¹/₂ tablespoons chopped thyme
1 bay leaf
2 tablespoons chopped flat-leaf
(Italian) parsley
toasted pine nuts, to serve (see Note)

SERVES 4

Rinse the wild rice and cook in a saucepan of plenty of boiling water for 25 minutes — it will only be partially cooked after this time. Drain.

When the rice is nearly done, pour the stock into a large saucepan with 375 ml (13 fl oz/1¹/₂ cups) water and bring to the boil. Reduce the heat to a simmer.

Meanwhile, finely chop the onion and slice the mushrooms. Melt the butter in a large heavy-based frying pan, add the onion and garlic and cook until the onion is softened but not browned. Add the white rice and stir until the rice grains are coated with butter, then stir in the mushrooms.

Add the wild rice, stock, thyme and bay leaf. Bring to the boil while stirring then reduce the heat, cover tightly with a lid and simmer for 15 minutes, or until the rice is tender and the stock has been absorbed.

Leave to stand for 5 minutes. Remove the bay leaf. Season then add the parsley and fluff up the rice with a fork. Sprinkle with pine nuts and serve.

PREPARATION TIME: 20 MINUTES +   COOKING TIME: 45 MINUTES

NOTE: Toast the pine nuts in a dry frying pan over medium heat, stirring constantly, until they are golden brown and fragrant. Watch carefully as they will burn easily.

TORTELLINI WITH EGGPLANT

1 red capsicum (pepper)
500 g (1 lb 2 oz) eggplant (aubergine)
500 g (1 lb 2 oz) fresh cheese and spinach tortellini
60 ml (2 fl oz/¼ cup) oil
2 garlic cloves, crushed
425 g (15 oz) tinned crushed tomatoes
250 ml (9 fl oz/1 cup) vegetable stock
25 g (1 oz) chopped basil

SERVES 4

Cut the red capsicum in half, remove the seeds and membrane and cut into small squares. Cut the eggplant into small cubes.

Cook the tortellini in a large saucepan of rapidly boiling salted water until *al dente*. Drain and return to the pan.

While the pasta is cooking, heat the oil in a large frying pan, add the garlic and red capsicum and stir over medium heat for 1 minute. Add the eggplant to the pan and stir gently over medium heat for 5 minutes, or until lightly browned.

Add the undrained tomatoes and vegetable stock to the pan. Stir and bring to the boil. Reduce the heat to low, cover the pan and cook for 10 minutes, or until the vegetables are tender. Add the basil and pasta and stir until mixed through.

PREPARATION TIME: 10 MINUTES   COOKING TIME: 20 MINUTES

NOTE: Cut the eggplant just before using, as it turns brown when exposed to the air.

PENNE WITH OLIVE
AND PISTACHIO PESTO

500 g (1 lb 2 oz) penne
125 g (4½ oz) pistachio nuts
4 garlic cloves
1 tablespoon green peppercorns
2 tablespoons lemon juice
150 g (5½ oz) pitted black olives
150 g (5½ oz/1½ cups) freshly grated parmesan cheese
125 ml (4 fl oz/½ cup) light olive oil
parmesan cheese shavings, to serve

SERVES 4

Cook the penne in a large saucepan of rapidly boiling salted water until *al dente*. Drain and return to the pan.

While the penne is cooking, combine the pistachio nuts, garlic, peppercorns, lemon juice, black olives and parmesan in a food processor for 30 seconds, or until roughly chopped.

While the motor is running, gradually pour in the olive oil in a thin stream. Blend until the mixture is smooth. Toss the pesto through the hot pasta and serve topped with the parmesan shavings.

PREPARATION TIME: 20 MINUTES   COOKING TIME: 10 MINUTES

Tortellini with eggplant

VEGETARIAN PHAD THAI

400 g (14 oz) flat rice stick noodles
1 small red capsicum (pepper)
6 spring onions (scallions)
100 g (3½ oz) fried tofu puffs
1 onion
60 ml (2 fl oz/¼ cup) soy sauce
2 tablespoons lime juice
1 tablespoon soft brown sugar
2 teaspoons sambal oelek (see Note)
2 tablespoons peanut oil
2 eggs, lightly beaten
2 garlic cloves, crushed
25 g (1 oz) chopped coriander (cilantro) leaves
90 g (3¼ oz/1 cup) bean sprouts, trimmed
40 g (1½ oz/¼ cup) chopped roasted peanuts

SERVES 4

Soak the noodles in warm water for 15–20 minutes, or until tender. Drain, then set aside.

Cut the capsicum in half, remove the seeds and membrane and cut into thin strips. Thinly slice the spring onions, diagonally. Cut the fried tofu puffs into 5 mm (¼ inch) wide strips. Cut the onion into thin wedges.

To make the stir-fry sauce, combine the soy sauce, lime juice, sugar and sambal oelek in a small bowl.

Heat a wok over high heat. Add enough peanut oil to coat the base and side. Add the egg and swirl to form a thin omelette. Cook for 30 seconds, or until just set. Remove from the wok, roll up, then thinly slice.

Heat the remaining oil in the wok. Add the onion, garlic and capsicum and cook over high heat for 2–3 minutes, or until the onion softens. Add the noodles, tossing well. Stir in the slices of omelette, the spring onion, tofu and half of the coriander. Pour in the stir-fry sauce, then toss to coat the noodles. Sprinkle with the bean sprouts and top with roasted peanuts and the remaining coriander. Serve immediately.

PREPARATION TIME: 20 MINUTES +   COOKING TIME: 5 MINUTES

NOTE: Sambal oelek is a Southeast Asian chilli paste.

JAMAICAN RICE WITH PEAS

400 g (14 oz/2 cups) long-grain rice
750 ml (26 fl oz/3 cups) coconut milk
400 g (14 oz) tinned kidney beans,
drained and rinsed (see Note)
2 teaspoons finely chopped thyme
4 garlic cloves, crushed
large pinch ground allspice
4 spring onions (scallions), bruised
1 small red chilli

SERVES 4–6

Combine all the ingredients in a large saucepan and add enough water to come about 2.5 cm (1 inch) above the rice. Slowly bring to the boil over medium heat, cover then reduce the heat to low and simmer for 25 minutes, or until the rice is tender and the liquid has been absorbed.

Remove the spring onion and chilli, season well and serve.

PREPARATION TIME: 5 MINUTES   COOKING TIME: 35 MINUTES

NOTE: This Jamaican staple is actually rice with beans; however beans are often referred to as peas in Jamaica. Kidney beans are commonly used, though some authentic versions contain hard-to-find gungo or pigeon peas.

CHILLI SATAY NOODLES

4 slender eggplants (aubergines)
500 g (1 lb 2 oz) thin fresh egg noodles
1 tablespoon oil
1 teaspoon sesame oil
50 g (1³/₄ oz/¹/₃ cup) peanuts
2 small red chillies
200 g (7 oz) sugar snap peas
100 g (3¹/₂ oz) bean sprouts, trimmed
60 g (2¹/₄ oz/¹/₄ cup) crunchy peanut
butter
1 tablespoon hoisin sauce
80 ml (2¹/₂ fl oz/¹/₃ cup) coconut milk
2 tablespoons lime juice
1 tablespoon Thai sweet chilli sauce

SERVES 4–6

Slice the eggplants. Add the noodles to a large saucepan of boiling water and cook for 3 minutes. Drain, rinse well under cold running water and drain again. Heat the oils in a wok or frying pan. Add the peanuts and toss over high heat for 1 minute, or until golden. Add the chillies, eggplant and sugar snap peas and cook over high heat for 2 minutes. Reduce the heat to medium and add the noodles and the sprouts. Toss for 1 minute, or until combined.

Blend the peanut butter, hoisin sauce, coconut milk, lime juice and chilli sauce until almost smooth. Add to the noodles. Toss over medium heat until the noodles are coated and the sauce is heated.

PREPARATION TIME: 10 MINUTES   COOKING TIME: 10 MINUTES

BUDDHIST VEGETARIAN NOODLES

15 g (¹/₂ oz) dried shiitake mushrooms
1 small carrot
150 g (5¹/₂ oz) baby corn
225 g (8 oz) tinned bamboo shoots
150 g (5¹/₂ oz) snow peas (mangetout)
¹/₂ small red capsicum (pepper)
1 small green capsicum (pepper)
40 g (1¹/₂ oz) Chinese cabbage
(wong bok)
400 g (14 oz) fresh flat egg noodles
2–3 tablespoons peanut or sunflower oil
90 g (3¹/₄ oz/1 cup) bean sprouts, trimmed
1 tablespoon thin strips fresh ginger
2 tablespoons vegetarian oyster sauce
(see Notes)
1 tablespoon mushroom soy sauce
(see Notes)
1 tablespoon light soy sauce
1 tablespoon Chinese rice wine
1 teaspoon sesame oil
ground white pepper, to taste
coriander (cilantro) leaves, to garnish

SERVES 4

Cover the mushrooms in boiling water and soak for 20 minutes. Drain. Discard the woody stalks and thinly slice the caps. Cut the carrot into thin batons. Quarter the baby corn lengthways. Drain the bamboo shoots and cut into thin batons. Cut the snow peas into thin batons. Cut the capsicums in half, remove the seeds and membrane and cut into thin batons. Finely shred the Chinese cabbage.

Cook the noodles in a large saucepan of boiling water for 1 minute, stirring to separate. Drain, rinse under cold running water and drain again.

Heat a wok over high heat, add 1 tablespoon of the peanut oil and swirl to coat the base and side. Stir-fry the carrot and corn for 1–2 minutes, then add the bamboo shoots and stir-fry for a further 1–2 minutes, or until just cooked but still crisp. Remove the vegetables from the wok.

Reheat the wok (add 2 teaspoons peanut oil if necessary) and add the snow peas and red and green capsicum. Stir-fry for 1–2 minutes, or until just cooked but still crisp. Add to the carrot and corn mixture. Reheat the wok (add another 2 teaspoons peanut oil if needed), then add the bean sprouts, Chinese cabbage and mushrooms and stir-fry for 30 seconds, or until wilted. Add the ginger and stir-fry for a further 1–2 minutes. Remove from the wok and add to the other vegetables.

Heat the remaining oil in the wok, and quickly stir-fry the noodles for 1–2 minutes, or until heated through, taking care not to let them break up. Stir in the vegetarian oyster sauce, mushroom soy sauce, light soy sauce and rice wine and stir thoroughly. Return all the vegetables to the wok and stir gently for 1–2 minutes, or until well combined with the noodles. Drizzle with the sesame oil, season with white pepper and garnish with the coriander leaves. Serve immediately.

PREPARATION TIME: 25 MINUTES +   COOKING TIME: 15 MINUTES

NOTES: Garlic, onions, spring onions and chillies have been omitted from this recipe because traditional Chinese vegetarians do not eat them.
Vegetarian oyster sauce and mushroom soy sauce are both available from Asian food stores.

GREEN PILAFF WITH CASHEWS

200 g (7 oz/4 cups) baby English spinach leaves
6 spring onions (scallions)
100 g (3½ oz/⅔ cup) cashew nuts, roughly chopped
2 tablespoons olive oil
2 garlic cloves, finely chopped
1 teaspoon fennel seeds
300 g (10½ oz/1½ cups) long-grain brown rice
2 tablespoons lemon juice
625 ml (21½ fl oz/2½ cups) vegetable stock
3 tablespoons chopped mint
3 tablespoons chopped flat-leaf (Italian) parsley

Preheat the oven to 180°C (350°F/Gas 4). Shred the English spinach into 1 cm (½ inch) pieces and chop the spring onion.

Put the cashew nuts on a baking tray and roast for 5–10 minutes, or until golden brown — watch them carefully so they don't burn.

Heat the oil in a large, deep frying pan and cook the spring onion over medium heat for 2 minutes, or until softened. Add the garlic and fennel seeds and cook for 1 minute, or until fragrant. Stir in the rice, mixing well to combine. Increase the heat to high, add the lemon juice, stock and 1 teaspoon salt and bring to the boil. Reduce the heat to low, cover with a tight-fitting lid and cook, without lifting the lid, for 45 minutes, or until the stock has been absorbed and the rice is cooked. Remove from the heat and sprinkle with the spinach and herbs. Stand, covered, for 8 minutes, then fork the spinach and herbs through the rice. Season. Serve sprinkled with cashews.

SERVES 6   PREPARATION TIME: 15 MINUTES   COOKING TIME: 1 HOUR 10 MINUTES

LINGUINE WITH ROASTED VEGETABLE SAUCE

4 large red capsicums (peppers)
500 g (1 lb 2 oz) firm ripe tomatoes
3 large red onions
1 bulb garlic
125 ml (4 fl oz/½ cup) balsamic vinegar
60 ml (2 fl oz/¼ cup) olive oil
2 teaspoons sea salt
2 teaspoons freshly ground black pepper
500 g (1 lb 2 oz) linguine
100 g (3½ oz) parmesan cheese, shaved
100 g (3½ oz) black olives

SERVES 4

Preheat the oven to 180°C (350°F/Gas 4). Cut the capsicums in half and remove the seeds and membrane. Cut the tomatoes and onions in half and separate and peel the garlic cloves.

Arrange the vegetables in a large ovenproof dish in a single layer. Pour the vinegar and oil over them and sprinkle with the sea salt and pepper. Bake for 50 minutes. Allow to cool for 5 minutes before puréeing in a food processor for 3 minutes, or until the mixture is smooth. Season with more salt and pepper, if necessary.

When the vegetables are almost cooked, cook the linguine in a large saucepan of rapidly boiling salted water until *al dente*. Drain. Serve the roasted vegetable sauce over the linguine with the parmesan cheese, olives and some extra black pepper.

PREPARATION TIME: 30 MINUTES   COOKING TIME: 50 MINUTES

Green pilaff with cashews

PUMPKIN GNOCCHI WITH SAGE BUTTER

500 g (1 lb 2 oz) pumpkin (winter squash), unpeeled
185 g (6^1/$_2$ oz/1^1/$_2$ cups) plain (all-purpose) flour
50 g (1^3/$_4$ oz/^{1}/$_2$ cup) freshly grated parmesan cheese
1 egg, beaten
100 g (3^1/$_2$ oz) butter
2 tablespoons chopped sage
sage leaves, to garnish

SERVES 4

Preheat the oven to 160°C (315°F/Gas 2–3). Brush a baking tray with oil or melted butter.

Cut the pumpkin into large pieces, leaving the skin on, and put on the tray. Bake for 1^1/$_4$ hours, or until very tender. Cool slightly. Scrape the flesh from the skin, avoiding any tough or crispy parts. Transfer to a large bowl. Sift the flour into the bowl, add half the parmesan, the egg and a little black pepper. After mixing thoroughly, turn onto a lightly floured surface and knead for 2 minutes, or until smooth.

Divide the dough in half. Using floured hands, roll each half into a sausage shape about 40 cm (16 inches) long. Cut into 16 equal pieces. Form each piece into an oval shape and press firmly with the floured prongs of a fork to make an indentation.

Lower batches of gnocchi into a large saucepan of boiling salted water. Cook for about 2 minutes, or until the gnocchi rise to the surface. Drain with a slotted spoon and keep them warm.

To make the sage butter, melt the butter in a small frying pan, remove from the heat and stir in the chopped sage.

To serve, divide the gnocchi among four serving bowls and drizzle with sage butter. Sprinkle with the remaining parmesan and garnish with sage leaves.

PREPARATION TIME: 45 MINUTES   COOKING TIME: 1 HOUR 30 MINUTES

PENNE WITH ROCKET

200 g (7 oz) rocket (arugula)
3 tomatoes
500 g (1 lb 2 oz) penne
100 g (3^1/$_2$ oz) butter
45 g (1^3/$_4$ oz/^{1}/$_2$ cup) freshly grated pecorino cheese
freshly grated parmesan cheese, to serve

SERVES 4

Roughly chop the rocket and finely chop the tomatoes.

Cook the penne in a large saucepan of rapidly boiling salted water until *al dente*. Drain and return to the pan. Place the pan over low heat. Add the butter, tossing it through until it melts and coats the pasta.

Add the rocket to the pasta along with the tomato. Toss through to wilt the rocket. Stir in the pecorino cheese and season to taste. Serve sprinkled with the parmesan cheese.

PREPARATION TIME: 15 MINUTES   COOKING TIME: 15 MINUTES

TAGLIATELLE WITH ASPARAGUS AND HERBS

500 g (1 lb 2 oz) tagliatelle
150 g (5^1/$_2$ oz) asparagus, woody ends trimmed
40 g (1^1/$_2$ oz) butter
1 tablespoon chopped flat-leaf (Italian) parsley
1 tablespoon chopped basil
310 ml (10^3/$_4$ fl oz/1^1/$_4$ cups) pouring (whipping) cream
50 g (1^3/$_4$ oz/^{1}/$_2$ cup) freshly grated parmesan cheese
parmesan cheese shavings, to serve

SERVES 4–6

Cook the tagliatelle in a large saucepan of rapidly boiling water until *al dente*. Drain and return to the pan.

While the pasta is cooking, cut the asparagus spears into short pieces. Heat the butter in a saucepan, add the asparagus and stir over medium heat for 2 minutes, or until just tender. Add the parsley, basil and cream and season. Cook for 2 minutes.

Add the parmesan cheese to the pan and stir well. When thoroughly mixed, add to the warm pasta and toss gently to distribute the ingredients evenly. Serve in warmed pasta bowls with shavings of parmesan cheese.

PREPARATION TIME: 15 MINUTES   COOKING TIME: 15 MINUTES

Penne with rocket

ASIAN MUSHROOM RISOTTO

10 g (1/4 oz) dried Chinese mushrooms
625 ml (21/2 fl oz/21/2 cups) boiling water
1 onion
500 ml (17 fl oz/2 cups) vegetable stock
2 tablespoons soy sauce
80 ml (21/2 fl oz/1/3 cup) mirin
150 g (51/2 oz) Swiss brown mushrooms
150 g (51/2 oz) oyster mushrooms
100 g (31/2 oz) fresh shiitake mushrooms
150 g (51/2 oz) shimeji mushrooms
40 g (11/2 oz) butter
1 tablespoon olive oil
3 garlic cloves, crushed
1 tablespoon finely chopped fresh ginger
440 g (151/2 oz/2 cups) arborio rice
100 g (31/2 oz) enoki mushrooms, trimmed
2 tablespoons snipped chives
parmesan cheese shavings, to garnish
(optional)

SERVES 4

Put the Chinese mushrooms in a bowl, cover with the boiling water and soak for 30 minutes, then drain, reserving the liquid. Remove and discard the stems and thinly slice the caps. Finely chop the onion.

Heat the vegetable stock, soy sauce, mirin, reserved mushroom liquid and 250 ml (9 fl oz/1 cup) water in a large saucepan, bring to the boil, then reduce the heat and keep at a low simmer, skimming off any scum that forms on the surface.

Trim and slice the Swiss brown, oyster and shiitake mushrooms, discarding any woody ends. Trim the shimeji mushrooms and pull apart into small clumps. Melt 1 tablespoon of the butter in a large saucepan over medium heat, add all the mushrooms except the Chinese and enoki and cook, stirring, for 3 minutes, or until wilted, then remove from the pan.

Heat the oil and remaining butter in the same saucepan over medium heat, add the onion and cook, stirring, for 4–5 minutes, or until the onion is soft and just starting to brown. Add the garlic and ginger and stir well until fragrant. Add the rice and stir for 1 minute, or until it is well coated in the oil mixture.

Gradually add 125 ml (4 fl oz/1/2 cup) of the hot stock to the rice. Stir constantly over medium heat until nearly all the liquid has been absorbed. Continue adding more stock, 125 ml (4 fl oz/1/2 cup) at a time, stirring constantly for 20–25 minutes, or until all of the stock has been absorbed and the rice is tender.

Add all the mushrooms and stir well. Season to taste. Garnish with the chives and shaved parmesan and serve.

PREPARATION TIME: 20 MINUTES + COOKING TIME: 45 MINUTES

NOODLES IN BLACK BEAN SAUCE

375 g (13 oz) thin fresh egg noodles
1 tablespoon dried, salted black beans, well rinsed (use Asian variety) (see Note)
3 spring onions (scallions)
1 teaspoon olive oil
1 teaspoon sesame oil
1 tablespoon grated fresh ginger
4 garlic cloves, crushed
2 tablespoons hoisin sauce
1 tablespoon black bean sauce
1 tablespoon sugar
125 ml (4 fl oz/½ cup) vegetable stock
235 g (8½ oz) tinned sliced bamboo shoots, drained

SERVES 4

Add the noodles to a large saucepan of boiling water and cook until just tender. Drain.

Chop the black beans and cut the spring onions into long slices.

Heat the oils in a wok or frying pan. Add the ginger and garlic and stir over low heat for 2 minutes. Add the black beans and stir for 2 minutes.

Add the hoisin and black bean sauces, sugar and stock to the pan. Simmer for 5 minutes until slightly reduced and thickened. Add the bamboo shoots, spring onion and noodles. Stir until heated through and all the ingredients are well combined. Serve immediately.

PREPARATION TIME: 10 MINUTES   COOKING TIME: 10–15 MINUTES

NOTE: Dried, salted black beans are available from Asian speciality food stores.

FUSILLI WITH SAGE AND GARLIC

500 g (1 lb 2 oz) fusilli
60 g (2¼ oz) butter
2 garlic cloves, crushed
10 g (¼ oz) sage leaves
2 tablespoons pouring (whipping) cream
freshly grated parmesan cheese, to serve

SERVES 4

Cook the fusilli in a large saucepan of rapidly boiling salted water until *al dente*. Drain and return to the pan.

While the pasta is cooking, melt the butter in a frying pan. Add the garlic and sage leaves. Cook over low heat for 4 minutes, stirring frequently.

Stir in the cream and season to taste. Stir the sauce through the pasta until thoroughly coated. Top each serving with freshly grated parmesan.

PREPARATION TIME: 10 MINUTES   COOKING TIME: 15 MINUTES

Noodles in black bean sauce

INDONESIAN COCONUT AND SPICE RICE

2 spring onions (scallions)
1 tablespoon oil
80 g (2³/₄ oz/¹/₂ cup) peanuts, roughly chopped
1 tablespoon shredded coconut
250 ml (9 fl oz/1 cup) coconut milk
10 cm (4 inch) lemon grass stem, white part only, lightly crushed with the side of a knife
8 curry leaves
1 teaspoon ground cumin
¹/₂ teaspoon ground cardamom
¹/₂ teaspoon ground turmeric
500 g (1 lb 2 oz/2¹/₂ cups) long-grain rice

SERVES 4

Cut the spring onions into 2.5 mm (¹/8 inch) slices.

Heat the oil in a wok. Add the peanuts and cook, stirring often, until they turn golden brown. Add the coconut and stir until it darkens slightly and becomes fragrant.

Pour the coconut milk and 500 ml (17 fl oz/2 cups) water into the wok. Add the lemon grass stem, curry leaves and spring onion then bring to the boil. Reduce the heat and simmer for 2 minutes. Add the cumin, cardamom and turmeric, and bring to the boil again. Lift out the lemon grass stem, then add the rice and cook until steam holes appear at the surface of the rice.

Cover the wok with a tight-fitting lid, reduce the heat to very low and cook for 10 minutes. Lift the lid, check if the rice is cooked, and continue cooking (with the lid on) if required.

PREPARATION TIME: 15 MINUTES   COOKING TIME: 20 MINUTES

NOTES: Basmati or jasmine rice can be used instead of long-grain rice, if you prefer.
　　Avoid lifting the lid of the wok while the rice is cooking, as all the steam will escape, resulting in thick, starchy rice.

EGG FRIED RICE

1 spring onion (scallion)
4 eggs
50 g (1³/4 oz/¹/3 cup) fresh or frozen peas (optional)
60 ml (2 fl oz/¹/4 cup) oil
550 g (1 lb 4 oz/3 cups) cold cooked white long-grain rice (you will need 200 g/7 oz/1 cup of uncooked rice)

SERVES 4

Chop the spring onion. Beat the eggs with a pinch of salt and 1 teaspoon of the spring onion. Cook the peas in a saucepan of simmering water for 3-4 minutes for fresh or 1 minute for frozen.

Heat a wok over high heat, add the oil and swirl to coat the base and side. Heat until very hot. Reduce the heat, add the egg and lightly scramble. Add the rice before the egg is set too hard, increase the heat and stir to separate the rice grains and break the egg into small bits. Add the peas and the remaining spring onion and season with salt. Stir constantly for 1 minute.

PREPARATION TIME: 15 MINUTES   COOKING TIME: 15 MINUTES

PUMPKIN AND PINE NUT TAGLIATELLE

1 large onion
750 g (1 lb 10 oz) butternut pumpkin (squash)
30 g (1 oz) butter
2 garlic cloves, crushed
375 ml (13 fl oz/1¹/2 cups) vegetable stock
¹/4 teaspoon ground nutmeg
250 ml (9 fl oz/1 cup) pouring (whipping) cream
500 g (1 lb 2 oz) fresh tagliatelle
80 g (2³/4 oz/¹/2 cup) pine nuts, toasted (see Note)
2 tablespoons snipped chives
freshly grated parmesan cheese, to serve

SERVES 4

Chop the onion. Chop the pumpkin into small pieces. Melt the butter in a large saucepan. Add the onion and cook for 3 minutes, or until soft and golden. Add the garlic and cook for another minute. Stir in the vegetable stock and add the pumpkin. Bring to the boil, reduce the heat slightly and cook until the pumpkin is tender. Reduce the heat to very low and season with the nutmeg and ¹/2 teaspoon black pepper. Stir in the cream until just warmed through — do not boil. Transfer to a food processor and process for about 30 seconds, until the mixture forms a smooth sauce.

Meanwhile, cook the tagliatelle in a large saucepan of rapidly boiling salted water until *al dente*. Drain and return to the pan. Return the sauce to the pan and gently reheat. Add to the pasta with the pine nuts and toss well. Serve sprinkled with chives and parmesan.

PREPARATION TIME: 25 MINUTES   COOKING TIME: 25 MINUTES

NOTE: Toast the pine nuts in a dry frying pan over medium heat, stirring constantly, until they are golden brown and fragrant. Watch carefully as they will burn easily.

Egg fried rice

ORIENTAL MUSHROOMS WITH HOKKEIN NOODLES

250 g (9 oz) hokkein (egg) noodles
1 red capsicum (pepper)
6 spring onions (scallions)
200 g (7 oz) shiitake mushrooms
1 teaspoon sesame oil
1 tablespoon peanut oil
2 garlic cloves, crushed
2 tablespoons grated fresh ginger
200 g (7 oz) oyster mushrooms
125 g (4^1/$_2$ oz) snipped garlic chives
40 g (1^1/$_2$ oz/^{1}/$_4$ cup) cashew nuts
2 tablespoons kecap manis (see Note)
60 ml (2 fl oz/^{1}/$_4$ cup) salt-reduced soy sauce

SERVES 4

Soak the hokkein noodles in boiling water for 2 minutes. Drain and set them aside.

Cut the red capsicum in half, remove the seeds and membrane and slice. Slice the spring onions and shiitake mushrooms.

Heat the oils in a wok and swirl to coat the base and side. Add the garlic, ginger and spring onion. Stir-fry over high heat for 2 minutes. Add the red capsicum and the oyster and shiitake mushrooms and stir-fry over high heat for 3 minutes, or until the mushrooms are golden brown.

Stir in the drained noodles. Add the chives, cashews, kecap manis and soy sauce. Stir-fry for 3 minutes, or until the noodles are coated in the sauce.

PREPARATION TIME: 35 MINUTES   COOKING TIME: 10 MINUTES

NOTE: Kecap manis is an Indonesian sweet soy sauce. If you are unable to find it, use soy sauce sweetened with a little soft brown sugar.

SPINACH AND RICOTTA GNOCCHI

4 slices white bread
125 ml (4 fl oz/$\frac{1}{2}$ cup) milk
500 g (1 lb 2 oz) frozen spinach, thawed
250 g (9 oz/1 cup) ricotta cheese
2 eggs
50 g (1$\frac{3}{4}$ oz/$\frac{1}{2}$ cup) freshly grated parmesan cheese
30 g (1 oz/$\frac{1}{4}$ cup) plain (all-purpose) flour
parmesan cheese shavings, to serve

SERVES 4–6

Remove the crust from the bread and soak the bread in the milk, in a shallow dish, for 10 minutes. Squeeze out all the excess liquid. Squeeze the excess liquid from the spinach.

Combine the bread in a bowl with the spinach, ricotta cheese, eggs and parmesan, then season. Use a fork to mix thoroughly. Cover and refrigerate for 1 hour.

Lightly dust your hands in flour. Roll heaped teaspoonsful of the mixture into dumplings. Lower batches of the gnocchi into a large saucepan of boiling salted water. Cook for about 2 minutes, or until the gnocchi rise to the surface. Transfer to serving plates. Drizzle with foaming butter, if you wish, and serve with the parmesan shavings.

PREPARATION TIME: 45 MINUTES +   COOKING TIME: 30 MINUTES

RICOTTA AND BASIL WITH TAGLIATELLE

500 g (1 lb 2 oz) tagliatelle
20 g ($\frac{3}{4}$ oz) flat-leaf (Italian) parsley
50 g (1$\frac{3}{4}$ oz) basil leaves
1 teaspoon olive oil
50 g (1$\frac{3}{4}$ oz) chopped sun-dried capsicum (pepper)
250 g (9 oz/1 cup) sour cream
250 g (9 oz/1 cup) ricotta cheese
25 g (1 oz/$\frac{1}{4}$ cup) freshly grated parmesan cheese

SERVES 4

Cook the tagliatelle in a large saucepan of rapidly boiling salted water until *al dente*. Drain and return to the pan.

While the pasta is cooking, process the parsley and basil in a food processor or blender until just chopped.

Heat the oil in a frying pan. Add the sun-dried capsicum and fry for 2–3 minutes. Stir in the sour cream, ricotta and parmesan and stir over low heat for 4 minutes, or until heated through. Do not allow to boil.

Add the herbs and sauce to the pasta, toss to combine and serve.

PREPARATION TIME: 15 MINUTES   COOKING TIME: 20 MINUTES

Spinach and ricotta gnocchi

PARSNIP GNOCCHI

500 g (1 lb 2 oz) parsnip
185 g (6$\frac{1}{2}$ oz/1$\frac{1}{2}$ cups) plain (all-purpose) flour
50 g (1$\frac{3}{4}$ oz/$\frac{1}{2}$ cup) freshly grated parmesan cheese

GARLIC HERB BUTTER
100 g (3$\frac{1}{2}$ oz) butter
2 garlic cloves, crushed
3 tablespoons chopped lemon thyme
1 tablespoon finely grated lime zest

SERVES 4

Cut the parsnip into large pieces. Cook in a large saucepan of boiling water for 30 minutes, or until very tender. Drain thoroughly and leave to cool slightly.

Mash the parsnip in a bowl until smooth. Sift the flour into the bowl and add half the parmesan. Season and mix to form a soft dough.

Divide the dough in half. Using floured hands, roll each half of the dough out on a lightly floured surface into a sausage shape 2 cm ($\frac{3}{4}$ inch) wide. Cut each sausage into short pieces, shape each piece into an oval and press the top gently with floured fork prongs.

Lower batches of gnocchi into a large saucepan of boiling salted water. Cook for about 2 minutes, or until the gnocchi rise to the surface. Use a slotted spoon to transfer to serving plates.

To make the garlic herb butter, combine all the ingredients in a small saucepan and cook over medium heat for 3 minutes, or until the butter is nutty brown.

To serve, drizzle the garlic herb butter over the gnocchi and sprinkle with the remaining parmesan cheese.

PREPARATION TIME: 45 MINUTES   COOKING TIME: 45 MINUTES

UDON NOODLE STIR-FRY

6 spring onions (scallions)
500 g (1 lb 2 oz) choy sum
2 carrots
150 g (5½ oz) snow peas (mangetout)
500 g (1 lb 2 oz) fresh udon noodles
2 tablespoons Japanese soy sauce
2 tablespoons mirin
2 tablespoons kecap manis (see Note)
1 tablespoon vegetable oil
3 garlic cloves, crushed
1 tablespoon grated fresh ginger
100 g (3½ oz) bean sprouts, trimmed
2 sheets roasted nori, cut into thin strips

SERVES 4

Cut the spring onions and choy sum into 5 cm (2 inch) lengths. Cut the carrot into 5 cm (2 inch) batons. Cut the snow peas in half, diagonally. Add the noodles to a saucepan of boiling water and cook for 1–2 minutes, or until tender and separated. Drain and rinse under hot water. Combine the soy sauce, mirin and kecap manis in a small bowl.

Heat a wok with a lid over high heat, add the oil and swirl to coat the base and side. Add the spring onion, garlic and ginger. Stir-fry for 1–2 minutes, or until softened. Add the carrot, snow peas and 1 tablespoon water, toss well, cover with the lid and cook for 1–2 minutes, or until the vegetables are just tender. Add the noodles, bean sprouts and choy sum, then pour in the sauce. Toss until the choy sum is wilted and coated with the sauce. Stir in the nori just before serving.

PREPARATION TIME: 15 MINUTES   COOKING TIME: 10 MINUTES

NOTE: Kecap manis is an Indonesian sweet soy sauce. If you are unable to find it, use soy sauce sweetened with a little soft brown sugar.

LINGUINE WITH RED CAPSICUM

1 large onion
3 red capsicums (peppers)
60 ml (2 fl oz/¼ cup) olive oil
2 garlic cloves, crushed
¼–½ teaspoon chilli powder or flakes
125 ml (4 fl oz/½ cup) pouring (whipping) cream
2 tablespoons chopped oregano
500 g (1 lb 2 oz) linguine or spaghetti (plain or spinach)

SERVES 6

Slice the onion. Cut the red capsicums into large flattish pieces and remove the seeds and membrane. Place, skin side up, under a hot grill (broiler) and cook for 8 minutes, or until black and blistered. Remove from the heat, cover with a damp tea towel (dish towel) and, when cool, peel away the skin and cut the flesh into thin strips.

Heat the oil in a large heavy-based saucepan. Add the onion and stir over low heat for 8 minutes, or until soft. Add the capsicum strips, garlic, chilli and cream and cook for 2 minutes, stirring occasionally. Add the oregano and season to taste.

About 15 minutes before the sauce is cooked, cook the pasta in a large saucepan of rapidly boiling salted water until *al dente*. Drain, and return to the pan. Add the sauce to the hot pasta and toss until well combined.

PREPARATION TIME: 20 MINUTES   COOKING TIME: 30 MINUTES

Udon noodle stir-fry

POTATO NOODLES WITH VEGETABLES

4 spring onions (scallions)
2 carrots
500 g (1 lb 2 oz) baby bok choy (pak choy)
or 250 g (9 oz) spinach
300 g (10½ oz) dried potato starch
noodles (see Notes)
10 g (¼ oz/⅓ cup) black fungus
(see Notes)
60 ml (2 fl oz/¼ cup) sesame oil
2 tablespoons vegetable oil
3 garlic cloves, finely chopped
4 cm (1½ inch) piece fresh ginger, grated
60 ml (2 fl oz/¼ cup) Japanese soy sauce
(see Notes)
2 tablespoons mirin
1 teaspoon sugar
2 tablespoons sesame and seaweed
sprinkle (see Notes)

SERVES 4

Finely chop two of the spring onions. Slice the remaining spring onions into 4 cm (1½ inch) pieces. Cut the carrots into 4 cm (1½ inch) batons. Roughly chop the baby bok choy.

Cook the noodles in a large saucepan of boiling water for about 5 minutes, or until they are translucent. Drain and rinse thoroughly under cold running water until the noodles are cold (this will also remove any excess starch). Use scissors to roughly chop the noodles into shorter lengths (this will make them easier to eat with chopsticks).

Pour hot water over the black fungus and soak for about 10 minutes.

Heat 1 tablespoon of the sesame oil with the vegetable oil in a large heavy-based frying pan or wok. Cook the garlic, ginger and finely chopped spring onion for 3 minutes over medium heat, stirring regularly. Add the carrots and stir-fry for 1 minute. Add the drained cooled noodles, sliced spring onion, bok choy, remaining sesame oil, soy sauce, mirin and sugar. Toss well to coat the noodles with the sauce. Cover and cook over low heat for 2 minutes. Add the drained fungus, then cover and cook for 2 minutes. Scatter over the sesame and seaweed sprinkle and serve immediately.

PREPARATION TIME: 25 MINUTES +   COOKING TIME: 25 MINUTES

NOTES : Potato starch noodles are also known as Korean pasta and are available from Asian food stores.

Dried black fungus, Japanese soy sauce and sesame and seaweed sprinkle are all available from Asian food stores.

RIGATONI WITH TOMATO, HALOUMI AND SPINACH

6 roma (plum) tomatoes
sugar, to sprinkle
4 garlic cloves, chopped
400 g (14 oz) rigatoni
60 ml (2 fl oz/¼ cup) lemon juice
60 ml (2 fl oz/¼ cup) olive oil
200 g (7 oz) haloumi cheese, thinly sliced
100 g (3½ oz/2 cups) baby English spinach

SERVES 6

Preheat the oven to 180°C (350°F/Gas 4). Cut the tomatoes in half and put on a non-stick baking tray, lined with foil if you like, and sprinkle generously with some sugar, salt, pepper and the garlic. Bake for 1 hour, or until quite dehydrated and shrunken. Leave to cool. Cut in half again.

While the tomatoes are cooking, cook the pasta in a large saucepan of rapidly boiling salted water until *al dente*. Drain, rinse under cold water and drain again. Allow to cool.

Combine the lemon juice and olive oil and season to taste. Toss the lemon dressing through the cooked, cold pasta and lightly toss through the tomato, haloumi cheese and spinach. Serve sprinkled with freshly cracked black pepper.

PREPARATION TIME: 30 MINUTES   COOKING TIME: 1 HOUR

SPINACH RAVIOLI WITH SUN-DRIED TOMATO SAUCE

150 g (5½ oz/¾ cup) firmly packed, chopped, cooked English spinach
250 g (9 oz/1 cup) ricotta cheese, well drained
2 tablespoons freshly grated parmesan cheese
1 tablespoon snipped chives
1 egg, lightly beaten
200 g (7 oz) packet round gow gee (egg) dumpling wrappers

SAUCE
100 g (3½ oz) sun-dried tomatoes
80 ml (2½ fl oz/⅓ cup) extra virgin olive oil
40 g (1½ oz/¼ cup) pine nuts

SERVES 4

Combine the spinach, ricotta, parmesan, chives and half the beaten egg in a bowl. Mix well and season to taste. Place 1½ teaspoons of the mixture into the centre of a gow gee wrapper. Brush the edge of the wrapper lightly with some of the remaining beaten egg, then cover with another wrapper. Repeat until all the wrappers are used. Press the edges firmly to seal. Using a 7 cm (2¾ inch) plain scone cutter, cut the ravioli into circles.

Cook the ravioli, in batches, in a large saucepan of rapidly boiling salted water for 4 minutes, or until *al dente*. Don't crowd the pan. Keep each batch warm while cooking the remainder. Carefully drain the ravioli, add to the sauce and toss very gently.

To make the sauce, slice the sun-dried tomatoes and combine with the other ingredients in a large saucepan. Heat slowly until warm.

PREPARATION TIME: 20 MINUTES   COOKING TIME: 15 MINUTES

Rigatoni with tomato, haloumi and spinach

RICOTTA-FILLED RAVIOLI WITH FRESH TOMATO SAUCE

RAVIOLI DOUGH
125 g (4^1/$_2$ oz/1 cup) plain
(all-purpose) flour
1 egg
1 tablespoon oil

FILLING
250 g (9 oz/1 cup) ricotta cheese
^{1}/$_2$ tablespoon chopped flat-leaf (Italian)
parsley
1 egg yolk

TOMATO SAUCE
1 kg (2 lb 4 oz) ripe tomatoes
1 onion
1 carrot
1 tablespoon olive oil
2 garlic cloves, crushed
50 g (1^3/$_4$ oz) tomato paste
(concentrated purée)
1 teaspoon soft brown sugar
125 ml (4 fl oz/^{1}/$_2$ cup) vegetable stock
1 tablespoon worcestershire sauce
30 g (1 oz) chopped basil
basil, extra, to garnish

SERVES 4–6

To make the ravioli dough, sift the flour into a bowl. Make a well in the centre, add the egg, oil and 1 teaspoon water and then gradually incorporate into the flour. Turn out onto a lightly floured board, knead until smooth and elastic. Cover and set aside for 30 minutes. While the pastry is resting, make the filling and the tomato sauce.

To make the filling, combine all the ingredients and mix well.

To make the tomato sauce, score a cross in the base of each tomato. Put in a heatproof bowl and cover with boiling water. Leave for 30 seconds, then transfer to cold water, drain and peel away the skin from the cross. Cut the tomatoes in half, scoop out the seeds and chop the flesh. Chop the onion and the carrot.

Heat the oil in a large heavy-based saucepan. Add the onion, carrot and garlic. Cook gently for 5–7 minutes. Add the tomatoes, tomato paste, sugar, stock, worcestershire sauce and basil. Bring to the boil, reduce to a simmer, then cover and cook for 30 minutes. Leave to cool slightly and then process the mixture in a food processor briefly. Keep warm.

Halve the ravioli dough and re-shape each piece into a smooth ball. Roll out each thinly to a long oblong shape. Place teaspoonsfuls of filling in mounds at 5 cm (2 inch) intervals in regular lines on one sheet of dough. Brush between the mounds with water and place the other sheet of dough carefully over the top. Press down between the filling to seal. Use a pastry wheel or knife to cut into squares.

Drop the ravioli into a saucepan of boiling water and cook for 8–10 minutes, or until tender. Remove the ravioli using a slotted spoon, and place into a heated serving dish. Spoon over the sauce, garnish with basil leaves and serve.

PREPARATION TIME: 35 MINUTES + COOKING TIME: 45–50 MINUTES

KHICHHARI

55 g (2 oz/¼ cup) yellow lentils
300 g (10½ oz/1½ cups) basmati rice
60 g (2¼ oz) ghee
1 teaspoon cumin seeds
6 whole cloves
½ cinnamon stick
2 onions, finely chopped
2 garlic cloves, finely chopped
2 cm (¾ inch) piece fresh ginger, finely chopped
1 teaspoon garam masala
60 ml (2 fl oz/¼ cup) lemon juice
750 ml (26 fl oz/3 cups) boiling water

SERVES 6

Soak the lentils in 500 ml (17 fl oz/2 cups) water in a large saucepan for 2 hours. Wash the rice in a sieve under cold water until the water from the rice runs clear. Drain.

Heat the ghee in a heavy-based saucepan over low heat and fry the cumin seeds, cloves and cinnamon stick for a few seconds. Increase the heat to medium, add the onion, garlic and ginger and cook for a few minutes until they soften and begin to brown.

Add the rice and lentils and toss to thoroughly coat in ghee. Add the garam masala, lemon juice, 1 teaspoon salt and the boiling water. Bring to the boil, reduce the heat to very low then cover tightly and cook for 15 minutes. Remove from the heat and gently fluff up with a fork. Cover the pan with a clean cloth and leave for 10 minutes. Fluff up again and season with salt to taste.

PREPARATION TIME: 10 MINUTES +   COOKING TIME: 25 MINUTES

SAFFRON RICE

500 g (1 lb 2 oz/2½ cups) long-grain rice
½ teaspoon saffron threads, crushed (see Note)
2 tablespoons olive oil
20 g (¾ oz) butter
60 g (2¼ oz) pistachio nuts, roughly chopped, to garnish (optional)

SERVES 6

Wash the rice in a sieve until the water runs clear, then drain well.

Bring 900 ml (32½ fl oz) water to the boil and add the saffron. Allow to infuse for 20 minutes.

Heat the oil in a heavy-based saucepan and add the rice, stirring well so that all the rice is coated evenly in the oil. Add the saffron water and ¼ teaspoon of salt and stir well. Bring to the boil and boil for 1 minute. Cover with a tight-fitting lid, then reduce the heat to as low as possible and cook for 10–12 minutes, or until all the water has been absorbed. Steam tunnels will form holes on the surface of the rice. Turn off the heat, then leave the pan covered for at least 10 minutes. Add the butter and fluff lightly with a fork. Garnish with pistachios and serve.

PREPARATION TIME: 5 MINUTES +   COOKING TIME: 15 MINUTES

NOTE: Because saffron is the main flavour in this recipe, it is important to use real saffron threads.

YOGHURT RICE

2 tablespoons urad dal (see Notes)
2 tablespoons chana dal (see Notes)
250 ml (9 fl oz/1 cup) boiling water
225 g (8 oz) basmati rice
2 tablespoons oil
1/2 teaspoon mustard seeds
12 curry leaves
3 dried chillies
1/4 teaspoon ground turmeric
pinch asafoetida (see Notes)
500 g (1 lb 2 oz/2 cups) thick plain yoghurt

SERVES 4

Soak the dals in the boiling water for 3 hours. Wash the rice under cold running water until the water runs clear. Drain.

Put the rice and 500 ml (17 fl oz/2 cups) water in a saucepan and bring rapidly to the boil. Stir, cover, reduce the heat to a slow simmer and cook for 10 minutes. Leave for 15 minutes before fluffing up with a fork.

Drain the dals and pat dry with paper towel. For the final seasoning, heat the oil in a small saucepan over low heat, add the mustard seeds then cover and shake the pan until the seeds start to pop. Add the curry leaves, dried chillies and dals and fry for 2 minutes, stirring occasionally. Lastly, stir in the turmeric and asafoetida.

Put the yoghurt in a large bowl, pour the fried dal mixture into the yoghurt and mix thoroughly. Mix the rice into the spicy yoghurt. Season with salt to taste. Serve cold, but before serving, stand the rice at room temperature for about 10 minutes.

PREPARATION TIME: 10 MINUTES +   COOKING TIME: 15 MINUTES

NOTES: In India, dal relates to any type of dried split pea, bean or lentil.

This is a popular dish to prepare for taking on journeys as the dish is served cold and the acid in the yoghurt acts as a preservative. Indians have developed special boxes of stackable enamel, tin or aluminium, called tiffin boxes, specially for carrying food.

Available as a yellowish powder or resin, asafoetida is made from the dried resin of a type of fennel. It is used as a flavour enhancer in Indian and Middle Eastern cooking.

RAVIOLI WITH HERBS

2 tablespoons olive oil
1 garlic clove, halved
800 g (1 lb 12 oz) ricotta-filled ravioli
60 g (2¼ oz) butter, chopped
2 tablespoons chopped flat-leaf
(Italian) parsley
20 g (¾ oz) chopped basil
2 tablespoons snipped chives
freshly grated parmesan cheese, to serve
(optional)

SERVES 6

Combine the oil and garlic in a small bowl, then set aside. Add the ravioli to a large saucepan of rapidly boiling salted water and cook until *al dente*.

Drain the ravioli in a colander and return to the pan. Add the oil to the pasta, discarding the garlic. Add the butter and herbs to the ravioli, toss well and season. Sprinkle with parmesan to serve.

PREPARATION TIME: 15 MINUTES   COOKING TIME: 5 MINUTES

NOTE: As a variation, use coriander (cilantro) instead of parsley.

LEMON AND DATE ZITI

360 g (12¾ oz/2 cups) dried stoned
dates, halved
375 ml (13 fl oz/1½ cups) port
375 g (13 oz) ziti
60 ml (2 fl oz/¼ cup) balsamic vinegar
125 ml (4 fl oz/½ cup) olive oil
150 g (5½ oz) rocket (arugula), trimmed
zest from 3 preserved lemons
(see Notes), finely chopped

SERVES 4–6

Place the dates and port in a saucepan. Bring to the boil, reduce the heat and simmer for 10 minutes. Strain the dates, reserving the port. Set aside to cool.

Cook the ziti in a large saucepan of rapidly boiling salted water until *al dente*. Drain, rinse in cold water and drain again. Allow to cool.

Combine the balsamic vinegar, reserved port and olive oil in a bowl. Season with a little sugar if necessary.

Toss the dressing through the pasta with the dates, rocket and lemon zest.

PREPARATION TIME: 15–20 MINUTES   COOKING TIME: 25 MINUTES

NOTES: Preserved lemons can be purchased at any good delicatessen or speciality food shop. They are available either per lemon or bottled.

TOMATO AND CHEESE RISOTTO CAKES

1 small onion
30 g (1 oz) sun-dried tomatoes
30 g (1 oz) mozzarella cheese
810 ml (28^1/$_4$ fl oz/3^1/$_4$ cups) vegetable stock
1 tablespoon olive oil
20 g (^{3}/$_4$ oz) butter
275 g (9^3/$_4$ oz/1^1/$_4$ cups) short-grain rice
35 g (1^1/$_4$ oz/^{1}/$_3$ cup) freshly grated parmesan cheese
oil, for deep-frying
70 g (2^1/$_2$ oz) mixed salad leaves, to serve

SERVES 6

Finely chop the onion. Chop the sun-dried tomatoes and cut the mozzarella cheese into 1 cm (^{1}/$_2$ inch) cubes.

Bring the stock to the boil in a small saucepan. Reduce the heat, cover and keep gently simmering. Heat the oil and butter in a heavy-based saucepan. Add the onion and stir over medium heat for 3 minutes, or until golden. Add the rice. Reduce the heat to low and stir for 3 minutes, or until the rice is lightly golden. Add a quarter of the stock to the pan. Stir for 5 minutes, or until all the liquid has been absorbed.

Repeat the process until all the stock has been added and the rice is almost tender, stirring constantly. Stir in the parmesan. Remove from the heat, transfer to a bowl to cool and refrigerate for 1 hour.

With wet hands, roll 2 tablespoons of rice mixture into a ball. Make an indentation in the ball and press in a cube of mozzarella and a couple of pieces of sun-dried tomato. Reshape the ball to cover the indentation then flatten slightly to a disc shape. Repeat the process with the remaining mixture. Refrigerate for 15 minutes.

Fill a deep-fryer or large heavy-based saucepan one-third full of oil and heat to 180°C (350°F), or until a cube of bread dropped in the oil browns in 15 seconds. Gently lower risotto cakes, a few at a time, into the oil. Cook for 1–2 minutes, or until golden brown. Remove with a slotted spoon and drain on paper towel. Serve the risotto cakes with fresh green salad leaves.

PREPARATION TIME: 30 MINUTES +   COOKING TIME: 40 MINUTES

FETTUCINE WITH GREEN OLIVES AND EGGPLANT

500 g (1 lb 2 oz) fettucine or tagliatelle
175 g (6 oz) green olives
1 large eggplant (aubergine)
2 tablespoons olive oil
2 garlic cloves, crushed
125 ml (4 fl oz/½ cup) lemon juice
2 tablespoons chopped flat-leaf (Italian) parsley
50 g (1¾ oz/½ cup) freshly grated parmesan cheese

SERVES 4

Cook the pasta in a large saucepan of rapidly boiling salted water until *al dente*. Drain and return to the pan.

While the pasta is cooking, slice the olives and cut the eggplant into small cubes.

Heat the oil in a heavy-based frying pan. Add the garlic and stir for 30 seconds. Add the eggplant and cook over medium heat, stirring frequently, for 6 minutes, or until tender. Add the olives, lemon juice and season to taste. Add the sauce to the pasta and toss. Sprinkle with the parsley and grated parmesan.

PREPARATION TIME: 20 MINUTES   COOKING TIME: 20 MINUTES

NOODLES WITH VEGETABLES AND HERBS

2 tomatoes
1 onion
1 celery stalk
1 small red chilli
1 carrot
30 g (1 oz) butter
1 tablespoon Taco seasoning mix
2 tablespoons tomato paste (concentrated purée)
125 ml (4 fl oz/½ cup) red wine
1 bay leaf
125 ml (4 fl oz/½ cup) vegetable stock
2 teaspoons chopped basil
2 teaspoons chopped flat-leaf (Italian) parsley
375 g (13 oz) thin fresh rice noodles

SERVES 4–6

Score a cross in the base of each tomato. Put in a heatproof bowl and cover with boiling water. Leave for 30 seconds, then transfer to cold water, drain and peel away the skin from the cross. Cut the tomatoes into wedges and remove the seeds. Slice the onion and celery. Cut the chilli in half, removed the seeds and cut into strips. Slice the carrot, diagonally.

Heat the butter and a little oil in a saucepan. Add the onion, chilli, celery and carrot and cook over medium heat for 5 minutes. Add the seasoning mix, tomato, tomato paste, wine, bay leaf and stock to the pan and bring to the boil. Reduce the heat to low and simmer, covered, for 15 minutes, stirring occasionally. Add the herbs to the sauce and stir until combined.

Cook the noodles in a large saucepan of boiling water until just tender, then drain. Toss with the sauce to serve.

PREPARATION TIME: 20 MINUTES   COOKING TIME: 25 MINUTES

Fettucine with green olives and eggplant

PULAO

500 g (1 lb 2 oz/2½ cups) basmati rice
1 teaspoon cumin seeds
2 onions
60 ml (2 fl oz/¼ cup) ghee or oil
2 tablespoons chopped almonds
2 tablespoons raisins or sultanas (golden raisins)
2 cinnamon sticks
5 cardamom pods
1 teaspoon sugar
1 tablespoon ginger juice
15 saffron threads, soaked in 1 tablespoon warm milk
2 Indian bay leaves (cassia leaves) (see Note)
250 ml (9 fl oz/1 cup) coconut milk
2 tablespoons fresh or frozen peas
rosewater (optional)

SERVES 6

Wash the rice in a sieve under cold, running water until the water from the rice runs clear. Drain the rice and put in a saucepan. Cover with water and soak for 30 minutes. Drain.

Dry-fry the cumin seeds in a small frying pan over low heat until aromatic. Thinly slice the onion.

Heat the ghee or oil in a karhai (Indian wok) or heavy-based frying pan and fry the almonds and raisins until browned. Remove from the pan, fry the onion in the same ghee until dark golden brown, then remove from the pan.

Add the rice, roasted cumin seeds, cinnamon, cardamom, sugar, ginger juice, saffron and some salt to the pan and fry for 2 minutes, or until aromatic.

Add the bay leaves and coconut milk to the pan, then add enough water to come about 5 cm (2 inches) above the rice. Bring to the boil, cover and cook over medium heat for 8 minutes, or until most of the water has evaporated.

Add the peas to the pan and stir well. Reduce the heat to very low and cook until the rice is cooked through. Stir in the fried almonds, raisins and onion, reserving some for garnishing. Drizzle with a few drops of rosewater if you would like a more perfumed dish. Garnish with the reserved almonds, raisins and onion, then serve.

PREPARATION TIME: 20 MINUTES   COOKING TIME: 15 MINUTES

NOTE: Indian bay leaves (cassia leaves) are available from Asian speciality food stores.

FETTUCINE WITH ZUCCHINI AND CRISP-FRIED BASIL

250 ml (9 fl oz/1 cup) olive oil
handful basil leaves
500 g (1 lb 2 oz) fettucine or tagliatelle
500 g (1 lb 2 oz) zucchini (courgettes)
60 g (2¼ oz) butter
2 garlic cloves, crushed
75 g (2¾ oz/¾ cup) freshly grated
parmesan cheese

SERVES 6

To crisp-fry the basil leaves, heat the oil in a small frying pan, add two leaves at a time and cook for 1 minute, or until crisp. Remove with a slotted spoon and drain on paper towel. Repeat with the remaining basil leaves.

Cook the fettucine in a large saucepan of rapidly boiling salted water until *al dente*. Drain and return to the pan.

While the pasta is cooking, grate the zucchini. Heat the butter in a deep heavy-based saucepan over low heat until the butter is foaming. Add the garlic and cook for 1 minute. Add the zucchini and cook, stirring occasionally, for 1–2 minutes or until softened. Add to the hot pasta. Add the parmesan and toss well. Serve the pasta garnished with the crisp basil leaves.

PREPARATION TIME: 15 MINUTES   COOKING TIME: 15 MINUTES

NOTE: The basil leaves can be fried up to 2 hours in advance. Store in an airtight container after cooling.

BLUE CHEESE TAGLIATELLE

2 zucchinis (courgettes)
30 g (1 oz) butter
1 garlic clove, crushed
100 ml (3½ fl oz) white wine
100 g (3½ oz) blue cheese, crumbled
300 ml (10½ fl oz) pouring
(whipping) cream
500 g (1 lb 2 oz) white or green tagliatelle
2–3 tablespoons freshly grated
parmesan cheese
chopped flat-leaf (Italian) parsley,
to garnish

SERVES 6

Slice the zucchini. Melt the butter in a frying pan. Add the zucchinis and garlic and cook until the zucchinis are tender. Stir in the wine, cheese, cream and a pinch of black pepper. Simmer for 10 minutes.

Meanwhile, cook the tagliatelle in a large saucepan of rapidly boiling salted water until *al dente*. Drain, rinse under warm water and drain again.

Return the pasta to the pan. Add the sauce and toss through the pasta for a few minutes over low heat. Serve sprinkled with the parmesan and parsley.

PREPARATION TIME: 15 MINUTES   COOKING TIME: 20 MINUTES

Fettucine with zucchini and crisp-fried basil

FETTUCINE WITH CREAMY MUSHROOM AND BEAN SAUCE

280 g (10 oz) fettucine
35 g (1^1/$_4$ oz/^{1}/$_4$ cup) sun-dried tomatoes
250 g (9 oz) green beans, trimmed
1 onion
250 g (9 oz) mushrooms
2 tablespoons oil
2 garlic cloves, crushed
125 ml (4 fl oz/^{1}/$_2$ cup) white wine
310 ml (10^3/$_4$ oz/1^1/$_4$ cups) pouring (whipping) cream
125 ml (4 fl oz/^{1}/$_2$ cup) vegetable stock
1 egg
3 tablespoons chopped basil
100 g (3^1/$_2$ oz/^{2}/$_3$ cup) pine nuts, toasted (See Note)
50 g (1^3/$_4$ oz) shaved parmesan cheese
herb sprigs, to serve (optional)

SERVES 4

Cook the fettucine in a large saucepan of rapidly boiling salted water until *al dente*. Drain, return to the pan and keep warm.

Cut the sun-dried tomatoes and beans into thin strips. Chop the onion and thinly slice the mushrooms.

Heat the oil in a large heavy-based frying pan. Add the onion and garlic and cook over medium heat for 3 minutes, or until softened. Add the sliced mushrooms and cook, stirring, for 1 minute. Add the wine, cream and stock. Bring to the boil then reduce the heat and simmer for 10 minutes.

Lightly beat the egg in a small bowl. Stirring constantly, add a little of the cooking liquid. Pour the mixture slowly into the pan, stirring constantly for 30 seconds. Keep the heat low because if the mixture boils, it will curdle.

Add the beans, basil, pine nuts and sun-dried tomato and stir until heated through, then season to taste.

Serve the sauce over the pasta. Garnish with the parmesan shavings and sprigs of fresh herbs, if desired.

PREPARATION TIME: 20 MINUTES   COOKING TIME: 20 MINUTES

NOTE: Toast the pine nuts in a dry frying pan over medium heat, stirring constantly, until they are golden brown and fragrant. Watch carefully as they will burn easily.

BROWN RICE AND PUY LENTILS WITH PINE NUTS AND SPINACH

2 tomatoes
1 red onion
1 carrot
2 celery stalks
200 g (7 oz/1 cup) long-grain brown rice
100 ml (3½ fl oz) extra virgin olive oil
2 garlic cloves, crushed
200 g (7 oz/1 cup) puy lentils
3 tablespoons chopped coriander (cilantro)
3 tablespoons chopped mint
2 tablespoons balsamic vinegar
1 tablespoon lemon juice
2 tablespoons pine nuts, toasted (see Note)
100 g (3½ oz/2 cups) baby English spinach leaves

SERVES 6–8

Score a cross in the base of each tomato. Put in a heatproof bowl and cover with boiling water. Leave for 30 seconds, then transfer to cold water, drain and peel away the skin from the cross. Cut the tomatoes in half, scoop out the seeds and dice the flesh. Dice the onion, carrot and celery. Bring a large saucepan of water to the boil. Add 1 teaspoon salt and the rice, and cook for 20 minutes, or until tender. Drain and refresh under cold water.

Heat 2 tablespoons of the oil in a saucepan and add the onion, garlic, carrot and celery. Cook over low heat for 5 minutes, or until softened, then add the puy lentils and 375 ml (13 fl oz/1½ cups) water. Bring to the boil and simmer for 15 minutes, or until tender. Drain well, but do not rinse. Combine with the rice, tomato, coriander and mint in a large bowl. Whisk the remaining oil with the vinegar and lemon juice and season well. Pour over the salad, add the pine nuts and English spinach, and toss to combine.

PREPARATION TIME: 15 MINUTES   COOKING TIME: 40 MINUTES

NOTE: Toast the pine nuts in a dry frying pan over medium heat, stirring constantly, until they are golden brown and fragrant.

BUCATINI WITH GORGONZOLA SAUCE

375 g (13 oz) bucatini or spaghetti
200 g (7 oz) gorgonzola cheese
1 celery stalk
20 g (¾ oz) butter
310 ml (10¾ fl oz/1¼ cups) pouring (whipping) cream
250 g (9 oz/1 cup) ricotta cheese, beaten until smooth

SERVES 6

Cook the bucatini in a large saucepan of rapidly boiling salted water until *al dente*. Drain and return to the pan.

While the pasta is cooking, chop the gorgonzola cheese into small cubes and chop the celery.

Heat the butter in a saucepan, add the celery and stir for 2 minutes. Add the cream, ricotta and gorgonzola and season to taste with freshly ground black pepper. Bring to the boil over low heat, stirring constantly, and then simmer for 1 minute. Add the sauce to the warm pasta and toss well.

PREPARATION TIME: 10 MINUTES   COOKING TIME: 20 MINUTES

Brown rice and puy lentils with pine nuts and spinach

VEGETABLE DONBURI

100 g (3½ oz) green beans
2 slender eggplants (aubergines)
1 onion
5 spring onions (scallions)
440 g (15½ oz/2 cups) Japanese short-grain rice
10 g (¼ oz) dried whole shiitake mushrooms
420 ml (14½ fl oz/1⅔ cups) boiling water
2 tablespoons oil
100 ml (3½ fl oz) Shoyu (Japanese soy sauce) (see Note)
100 ml (3½ fl oz) mirin
55 g (2 oz/¼ cup) sugar
4 eggs, lightly beaten

SERVES 4

Trim the green beans and cut them into 4 cm (1½ inch) lengths. Slice the eggplants diagonally and cut the spring onions into 2 cm (¾ inch) lengths. Slice the onion.

Wash the rice and put in a saucepan with 625 ml (21½ fl oz/2½ cups) water. Bring to the boil then reduce the heat and simmer, covered, for 15 minutes. Leave, covered, for 10 minutes.

Meanwhile, soak the mushrooms in the boiling water for 15 minutes. Drain and reserve the soaking liquid. Remove the stems and cut the caps in half.

Heat the oil in a deep frying pan. Cook the onion over medium heat for 4 minutes, or until softened but not browned. Add the eggplant and cook for 3–4 minutes, or until softened. Add the beans, mushrooms and spring onion and cook for 2–3 minutes, or until almost cooked. Combine the Shoyu, mushroom soaking liquid, mirin and sugar, and stir through the vegetables. Simmer for 4 minutes.

Pour the egg over the vegetables, cover and simmer for 1 minute, or until partly cooked. Serve the rice in bowls, spoon on the vegetable mixture and pour on the cooking sauce.

PREPARATION TIME: 20 MINUTES +   COOKING TIME: 35 MINUTES

NOTE: Shoyu (Japanese soy sauce) is available from Asian speciality food stores.

ONION AND PARMESAN PILAFF

3 onions
60 g (2¼ oz) butter
2 garlic cloves, crushed
400 g (14 oz/2 cups) basmati rice
1.25 litres (44 fl oz/5 cups) vegetable stock
235 g (8½ oz/1½ cups) peas
50 g (1¾ oz/½ cup) freshly grated parmesan cheese
30 g (1 oz) chopped flat-leaf (Italian) parsley

SERVES 6

Chop the onions. Melt the butter in a large saucepan, add the onion and garlic and stir over low heat for 5 minutes, or until soft and golden. Add the rice and stock, bring to the boil and stir once. Reduce the heat to low and simmer, uncovered, for 5 minutes or until almost all the liquid has been absorbed.

Add the peas and stir until combined. Cover the pan and cook over very low heat for 10 minutes, or until the rice is tender. Stir in the parmesan cheese and parsley and serve.

PREPARATION TIME: 5 MINUTES   COOKING TIME: 30 MINUTES

MUSHROOM RISOTTO FRITTERS

1 small onion
150 g (5½ oz) small button mushrooms
800 ml (28 fl oz) vegetable stock
1 tablespoon olive oil
20 g (¾ oz) butter
220 g (7¾ oz/1 cup) arborio or short-grain rice
35 g (1¼ oz/⅓ cup) freshly grated parmesan cheese
oil, for pan-frying

SERVES 4

Finely chop the onion and thinly slice the mushrooms. Bring the stock to the boil in a small saucepan. Reduce the heat, cover and simmer slowly until needed. Heat the oil and butter in a heavy-based saucepan. Add the onion, stir over medium heat for 3 minutes, or until softened. Add the rice, cook for 2 minutes. Add the mushrooms, cook for 3 minutes, or until soft. Add the hot stock, 125 ml (4 fl oz/½ cup) at a time, stirring constantly, until all the stock has been added, absorbed and the rice is just tender and creamy. (This will take about 20 minutes.) Stir in the parmesan cheese and remove from the heat.

Transfer the mixture to a bowl to cool, then refrigerate for at least 1 hour. With wet hands, shape small handfuls of mixture into flat rounds. Chill for 15 minutes. Heat 2.5 cm (1 inch) oil in a non-stick frying pan. Cook the fritters for 3–4 minutes each side, until golden and crisp. Drain on paper towel.

PREPARATION TIME: 20 MINUTES +   COOKING TIME: 35–40 MINUTES

Onion and parmesan pilaff

CHILLI CASHEW NOODLES

200 g (7 oz) thin noodles
3 red chillies
1 red capsicum (pepper)
2 celery stalks
2 teaspoons chilli oil
60 ml (2 fl oz/¼ cup) oil
80 g (2¾ oz/½ cup) roasted cashew nuts
2 tablespoons chopped spring onions (scallions)
225 g (8 oz) tinned whole baby corn, drained
100 g (3½ oz) bean sprouts, trimmed
1 tablespoon soy sauce
2 tablespoons Thai sweet chilli sauce

Chop the noodles, then add them to a large saucepan of simmering water and cook until just tender, then drain.

Cut the chillies into strips. Cut the red capsicum in half, remove the seeds and membrane and thinly slice. Slice the celery stalks diagonally.

Heat the oils in a wok or frying pan, add the chilli and cook over medium heat for 1 minute. Add the cashews and toss for 1 minute, or until golden.

Add the spring onion, corn and sprouts to the pan and cook over medium heat for 3 minutes, or until tender.

Stir in the noodles and combined soy and Thai sweet chilli sauces. Toss until the noodles are heated through and the ingredients are combined. Serve.

SERVES 4   PREPARATION TIME: 15 MINUTES   COOKING TIME: 10 MINUTES

CASSEROLES, CURRIES STIR-FRIES AND BAKES

INDIVIDUAL VEGETABLE POT PIES

1 potato
150 g (5^1/$_2$ oz) pumpkin (winter squash)
1 large carrot
1 onion
1 red capsicum (pepper)
150 g (5^1/$_2$ oz) small broccoli florets
1 tablespoon oil
50 g (1^3/$_4$ oz) butter
2 tablespoons plain (all-purpose) flour
375 ml (13 fl oz/1^1/$_2$ cups) milk
125 g (4^1/$_2$ oz/1 cup) grated cheddar cheese
2 egg yolks
cayenne pepper, to taste
2 sheets ready-rolled puff pastry
1 egg, lightly beaten
1 teaspoon poppy seeds

SERVES 6

Cut the potato into small cubes. Cut the pumpkin and the carrot into 1 cm (^{1}/$_2$ inch) cubes. Finely chop the onion. Cut the red capsicum in half, remove the seeds and membrane and cut into 1 cm (^{1}/$_2$ inch) squares.

Preheat the oven to 210°C (415°F/Gas 6–7). Brush six 250 ml (9 fl oz/1 cup) capacity ramekins or dariole moulds with oil. Steam or microwave the potato, pumpkin, carrot and broccoli until just tender. Drain well and place in a large bowl. Heat the oil in a frying pan and cook the onion and red capsicum over medium heat for 2 minutes until soft. Add to the bowl.

Heat the butter in a saucepan and add the flour. Stir over low heat for 2 minutes, or until lightly golden. Add the milk gradually, stirring until smooth. Stir over medium heat for 3 minutes, or until the mixture boils and thickens. Boil for another minute, then remove from the heat and cool slightly. Add the cheese and egg yolks to the sauce and stir to combine. Season to taste with cayenne pepper and salt.

Add the sauce to the vegetables and stir to combine. Divide between the ramekins. Cut six circles from the pastry to fit the top of the ramekins and press the edges to seal. Brush with beaten egg and sprinkle with poppy seeds. Bake for 30 minutes, or until golden brown.

PREPARATION TIME: 40 MINUTES   COOKING TIME: 45 MINUTES

NOTE: These pies are best eaten on the day they are made.

LIMA BEAN CASSEROLE

185 g (6½ oz/1 cup) dried lima beans
1 large onion
1 small carrot
1 small celery stalk
60 ml (2 fl oz/¼ cup) olive oil
1 garlic clove, chopped
400 g (14 oz) tinned good-quality crushed tomatoes
1 tablespoon tomato paste (concentrated purée)
2 teaspoons chopped dill
extra virgin olive oil, for serving

SERVES 6–8

Cover the lima beans with plenty of cold water and leave to soak overnight. Drain well.

Bring a large saucepan of water to the boil, add the beans and return to the boil, then reduce the heat to medium and cook, partially covered, for 45–60 minutes, or until the beans are tender but not mushy. Drain. Preheat the oven to 180°C (350°F/Gas 4).

Slice the onion and chop the carrot and celery. Heat the oil in a 2.5 litre (88 fl oz/10 cup) flameproof casserole dish over medium heat. Add the onion, garlic, carrot and celery, and cook for 5 minutes, or until the onion is translucent. Add the tomatoes, tomato paste and 125 ml (4 fl oz/½ cup) water. Bring to the boil, then reduce the heat and simmer for 3 minutes.

Add the lima beans and dill to the casserole dish, then season to taste. Bring back to the boil, then cover and bake for 50 minutes, or until the sauce is thick and the lima beans are soft. Serve hot or at room temperature, drizzled with the oil.

PREPARATION TIME: 20 MINUTES +   COOKING TIME: 2 HOURS

PUMPKIN CURRY

1 onion
800 g (1 lb 12 oz) pumpkin (winter squash)
2 tablespoons sesame seeds
1 tablespoon peanut oil
3 garlic cloves, crushed
2 teaspoons finely chopped fresh ginger
1 teaspoon ground coriander
2 teaspoons ground cumin
2 teaspoons finely chopped red chilli
250 ml (9 fl oz/1 cup) coconut cream
250 ml (9 fl oz/1 cup) vegetable stock
2 tablespoons coriander (cilantro) leaves

SERVES 4

Finely chop the onion. Cut the pumpkin into 2 cm (¾ inch) cubes. Heat a wok to hot. Stir-fry the sesame seeds for 1–2 minutes, or until toasted. Remove. Add the oil to the wok and swirl to coat the base and side. Stir-fry the onion for 3 minutes, or until soft. Add the garlic, ginger, spices and chilli, and cook for 1 minute, or until fragrant.

Add the pumpkin, stir-fry for 1 minute, then pour in the coconut cream and stock and bring to the boil. Reduce the heat and simmer, loosely covered, for 10 minutes. Uncover and simmer for a further 5–10 minutes, or until the pumpkin is tender and the liquid has thickened. Season with salt and scatter with the sesame seeds and coriander.

PREPARATION TIME: 20 MINUTES   COOKING TIME: 30 MINUTES

PEA, EGG AND RICOTTA CURRY

4 hard-boiled eggs

1/2 teaspoon ground turmeric

2 small onions

25 g (4 1/2 oz) baked ricotta cheese (see Note)

45 ml (1 1/2 fl oz) ghee or oil

1 bay leaf

1 teaspoon finely chopped garlic

1 1/2 teaspoons ground coriander

1 1/2 teaspoons garam masala

1/2 teaspoon chilli powder (optional)

125 g (4 1/2 oz/ 1/2 cup) tinned peeled, chopped tomatoes

1 tablespoon tomato paste (concentrated purée)

1 tablespoon plain yoghurt

80 g (2 3/4 oz/ 1/2 cup) frozen peas

2 tablespoons finely chopped coriander (cilantro) leaves

SERVES 4

Peel the eggs and coat them with the turmeric. Finely chop the onion and cut the ricotta into 1 cm (1/2 inch) cubes.

Melt the ghee in a large saucepan and cook the eggs over moderate heat for 2 minutes until they are light brown, stirring constantly. Set aside.

Add the bay leaf, onion and garlic to the pan and cook over moderately high heat, stirring frequently, until the mixture is well-reduced and pale gold. Lower the heat if the mixture is browning too quickly. Add the coriander, garam masala and chilli powder, if using, and cook until fragrant.

Add the tomatoes, tomato paste and 125 ml (4 fl oz/ 1/2 cup) water. Cover and simmer for 5 minutes. Return the eggs to the pan with the ricotta, yoghurt, peas and 1/4 teaspoon salt and cook for 5 minutes. Remove the bay leaf, sprinkle with the coriander and serve immediately.

PREPARATION TIME: 15 MINUTES   COOKING TIME: 30 MINUTES

NOTE: Baked ricotta cheese is available from delicatessens and some supermarkets, but it is easy enough to prepare your own. Preheat the oven to 160°C (315°F/Gas 2–3). Slice the required amount of fresh ricotta (not cottage cheese or blended ricotta) into 3 cm (1 1/4 inch) thick slices. Place the ricotta on a lightly greased baking tray and bake for 25 minutes.

CHICKPEA CURRY

2 onions
1 tablespoon ghee or oil
4 garlic cloves, crushed
1 teaspoon chilli powder
1 teaspoon turmeric
1 teaspoon paprika
1 tablespoon ground cumin
1 tablespoon ground coriander
2 x 440 g (15½ oz) tins chickpeas, drained
440 g (15½ oz) tinned chopped tomatoes
1 teaspoon garam masala

SERVES 4

Thinly slice the onions. Heat the ghee or oil in a frying pan. Add the onion and garlic to the pan and cook over medium heat, stirring, until soft.

Add the chilli powder, turmeric, paprika, cumin, coriander and 1 teaspoon salt. Stir for 1 minute.

Add the chickpeas and undrained tomatoes and stir until combined. Simmer, covered, over low heat for 20 minutes, stirring occasionally. Stir in the garam masala. Simmer, covered, for another 10 minutes.

PREPARATION TIME: 15 MINUTES   COOKING TIME: 45 MINUTES

NOTE: This curry makes a delicious meal wrapped inside chapattis or naan bread.

CASHEW NUT CURRY

1 onion
2 green chillies
1 pandanus leaf (see Note)
750 ml (26 fl oz/3 cups) coconut milk
1 tablespoon grated fresh ginger
½ teaspoon ground turmeric
3 cm (1¼ inch) piece fresh galangal
8 curry leaves
1 cinnamon stick
250 g (9 oz) cashew nuts
2 tablespoons chopped coriander (cilantro) leaves

SERVES 6 AS PART OF A SHARED MEAL

Chop the onion. Cut the chillies in half, remove the seeds and finely chop. Shred the pandanus leaf lengthways into about three sections, and tie into a large knot.

Combine the coconut milk, onion, ginger, turmeric, galangal, chilli, curry leaves, cinnamon stick and pandanus leaf in a saucepan and bring to the boil. Reduce the heat and simmer for 20 minutes. Add the cashew nuts, and cook for a further 30 minutes, or until the nuts are tender.

Remove from the heat and discard the galangal, cinnamon stick and pandanus leaf. Sprinkle over the coriander and serve with rice and a couple of other dishes.

PREPARATION TIME: 15 MINUTES   COOKING TIME: 55 MINUTES

NOTE: Popular in Southeast Asian cooking, pandanus leaves are most often used to flavour rice dishes. They are available from Asian speciality food stores.

VEGETABLE LASAGNE

3 large red capsicums (peppers)
1 large onion
500 g (1 lb 2 oz) English spinach
500 g (1 lb 2 oz) mushrooms
90 g (3¼ oz) sun-dried tomatoes
2 large eggplants (aubergines)
2 tablespoons oil
3 garlic cloves, crushed
1 teaspoon dried mixed herbs
1 teaspoon dried oregano
440 g (15½ oz) tinned crushed tomatoes
440 g (15½ oz) tinned red kidney beans, drained
1 tablespoon sweet chilli sauce
250 g (9 oz) packet instant lasagne
30 g (1 oz) basil leaves
25 g (1 oz/¼ cup) grated parmesan cheese
30 g (1 oz/¼ cup) grated cheddar cheese

CHEESE SAUCE
60 g (2¼ oz) butter
30 g (1 oz/¼ cup) plain (all-purpose) flour
500 ml (17 fl oz/2 cups) milk
600 g (1 lb 5 oz) ricotta cheese

SERVES 6

Preheat the oven to 180°C (350°F/Gas 4). Brush a 28 x 35 cm (11¼ x 14 inch) ovenproof dish with oil.

Cut the red capsicum in half, remove the seeds and membrane and cut into large flattish pieces. Cook, skin side up, under a hot grill (broiler) for 8 minutes, or until the skin is black and blistered. Cover with a damp tea towel (dish towel) and when cool, peel away the skin and cut the flesh into long thin strips. Set aside. Chop the onion and the English spinach. Slice the mushrooms and the sun-dried tomatoes.

Slice the eggplant into 1 cm (½ inch) rounds and put in a large saucepan of boiling water. Cook for 1 minute, or until just tender. Drain, pat dry with paper towel and set aside.

Heat the oil in a large heavy-based frying pan and add the onion, garlic and herbs. Cook over medium heat for 5 minutes, or until the onion is soft. Add the sliced mushrooms and cook for 1 minute.

Add the crushed tomatoes, red kidney beans, chilli sauce and season to taste. Bring to the boil, reduce the heat and simmer for 15 minutes, or until the sauce thickens. Remove from the heat and set aside.

To make the cheese sauce, heat the butter in a saucepan and stir in the flour over medium heat for 1 minute, or until smooth. Remove from the heat and gradually stir in the milk. Return to the heat and stir constantly until the sauce boils and begins to thicken. Simmer for another minute. Add the ricotta and stir until smooth.

Dip the lasagne sheets, if necessary, in hot water to soften slightly and arrange four sheets on the base of the prepared dish. Build up layers on top of the pasta, using half of the eggplant, the spinach, the basil, the grilled capsicum strips, the mushroom sauce and then the sun-dried tomatoes. Top with a layer of pasta and press gently. Repeat the layers, finishing with a layer of lasagne. Top with the cheese sauce and sprinkle with the combined parmesan and cheddar cheeses. Bake for 45 minutes, or until the pasta is soft.

PREPARATION TIME: 40 MINUTES   COOKING TIME: 1 HOUR 15 MINUTES

ASIAN GREENS WITH TERIYAKI TOFU DRESSING

650 g (1 lb 7 oz) baby bok choy (pak choy)

500 g (1 lb 2 oz) choy sum

440 g (15 1/2 oz) snake (yard-long) beans, topped and tailed

1 onion

60 ml (2 fl oz/1/4 cup) vegetable oil

60 g (2 1/4 oz/1/3 cup) soft brown sugar

1/2 teaspoon chilli powder

2 tablespoons grated fresh ginger

250 ml (9 fl oz/1 cup) teriyaki sauce

1 tablespoon sesame oil

600 g (1 lb 5 oz) silken firm tofu, drained

SERVES 6

Cut the baby bok choy and choy sum widthways into thirds. Cut the snake beans into 10 cm (4 inch) lengths. Thinly slice the onion. Heat a wok over high heat, add 1 tablespoon of the oil and swirl to coat the base and side. Cook the onion for 3–5 minutes, or until crisp. Remove with a slotted spoon and drain on paper towel.

Reheat the wok over high heat and add 1 tablespoon of the oil. Add half the greens and stir-fry for 2–3 minutes, or until wilted. Remove from the wok. Repeat with the remaining oil and greens. Drain any liquid from the wok.

Add the combined sugar, chilli powder, ginger and teriyaki sauce to the wok, then bring to the boil. Simmer for 1 minute. Add the sesame oil and tofu and simmer for 2 minutes, turning once — the tofu will break up. Divide the greens among six serving plates, then top with the dressing. Sprinkle with the fried onion.

PREPARATION TIME: 15 MINUTES   COOKING TIME: 20 MINUTES

COMBINATION VEGETABLE STEW

1 small onion

2 small carrots

2 zucchinis (courgettes)

320 g (11 oz) cauliflower

20 green beans

2 teaspoons olive oil

60 g (2 1/4 oz/1/4 cup) tomato paste (concentrated purée)

1/4 teaspoon chilli powder

1 teaspoon cumin seeds

125 ml (4 fl oz/1/2 cup) tomato juice

250 ml (9 fl oz/1 cup) vegetable stock

440 g (15 1/2 oz) tinned tomatoes, crushed

SERVES 4–6

Thinly slice the onion. Slice the carrots and cut the zucchinis into chunks. Cut the cauliflower into small florets and top and tail the beans.

Heat the oil in a large saucepan. Add the onions, tomato paste, chilli powder, cumin seeds and tomato juice. Stir until well combined.

Add the stock and crushed tomatoes. Bring to the boil. Reduce the heat, add the remaining vegetables and simmer, uncovered, until soft. Serve with fresh tortillas.

PREPARATION TIME: 15 MINUTES   COOKING TIME: 10–15 MINUTES

Asian greens with teriyaki tofu dressing

SWEET AND SOUR TOFU

1 large carrot
6–8 spring onions (scallions)
100 g (3½ oz) snow peas (mangetout)
80 ml (2½ fl oz/⅓ cup) rice vinegar
2 tablespoons light soy sauce
1½ tablespoons caster (superfine) sugar
2 tablespoons tomato sauce (ketchup)
375 ml (13 fl oz/1½ cups) vegetable stock
600 g (1 lb 5 oz) firm tofu
60–80 ml (2–2½ fl oz/¼–⅓ cup) vegetable oil
185 g (6½ oz/2 cups) bean sprouts or soy bean sprouts, trimmed
90 g (3¼ oz/1 cup) sliced button mushrooms
1 tablespoon cornflour (cornstarch) dissolved in 2 tablespoons water

SERVES 4

Cut the carrot into thin batons. Slice the spring onion diagonally. Halve the snow peas diagonally.

Combine the vinegar, soy sauce, sugar, tomato sauce and vegetable stock in a small bowl.

Cut the tofu in half horizontally, then cut into 16 triangles in total. Heat a wok over high heat, add 2 tablespoons of the oil and swirl to coat the base and side. Add the tofu in batches and stir-fry over medium heat for 2 minutes on each side, or until crisp and golden. Drain on paper towel and set aside. Keep warm.

Wipe the wok clean, then reheat over high heat. Add the remaining oil and swirl to coat the base and side. Add the carrot, bean sprouts, mushrooms, spring onion and snow peas and stir-fry for 1 minute. Add the sauce and stir for 1 minute. Add the cornflour paste and cook until the sauce thickens.

Divide the tofu among the serving bowls and spoon some sauce over the top. Serve with steamed rice.

PREPARATION TIME: 15 MINUTES   COOKING TIME: 20 MINUTES

ORANGE SWEET POTATO AND SPINACH STIR-FRY

500 g (1 lb 2 oz) orange sweet potato
225 g (8 oz) tinned water chestnuts
1 tablespoon vegetable oil
2 garlic cloves, crushed
2 teaspoons sambal oelek (see Note)
2 teaspoons grated palm sugar (jaggery) or soft brown sugar
390 g (13³/4 oz) English spinach, stems removed
2 tablespoons soy sauce
2 tablespoons vegetable stock

Cut the sweet potato into 1.5 cm (⁵/8 inch) cubes. Cook in a large saucepan of boiling water for 15 minutes, or until tender. Drain well. Slice the water chestnuts.

Heat a wok over high heat, add the oil and swirl to coat the base and side. Stir-fry the garlic and sambal oelek for 1 minute, or until fragrant. Add the sweet potato and water chestnuts and stir-fry over medium–high heat for 2 minutes. Reduce the heat to medium, add the palm sugar and cook for a further 2 minutes, or until the sugar has melted. Add the spinach, soy sauce and stock and toss until the spinach has just wilted. Serve with steamed rice.

SERVES 4   PREPARATION TIME: 15 MINUTES   COOKING TIME: 20 MINUTES

NOTE: Sambal oelek is a Southeast Asian chilli paste.

VEGETABLE KORMA

3 tomatoes
1 onion
300 g (10¹/2 oz) cauliflower
300 g (10¹/2 oz) pumpkin (winter squash)
3 slender eggplants (aubergines)
2 carrots
125 g (4¹/2 oz) green beans
2 tablespoons oil
2 tablespoons ready-made green masala paste
1 teaspoon chilli powder
1 tablespoon grated fresh ginger
375 ml (13 fl oz/1¹/2 cups) vegetable stock

SERVES 4–6

Score a cross in the base of each tomato. Put in a heatproof bowl and cover with boiling water. Leave for 30 seconds, then transfer to cold water, drain and peel away the skin from the cross. Cut the tomatoes in half, scoop out the seeds and chop the flesh. Chop the onion. Cut the cauliflower into florets. Cut the pumpkin, eggplants and carrots into large pieces. Trim and chop the beans.

Heat the oil in a large heavy-based saucepan. Add the masala paste and cook over medium heat for 2 minutes, or until the oil begins to separate from the paste. Add the chilli powder, ginger and onion, and cook for 3 minutes, or until the onion softens.

Add the cauliflower, pumpkin, eggplant and carrot and stir to coat in the paste mixture. Stir in the tomato and stock and bring to the boil, then reduce the heat and simmer, uncovered, for 30 minutes. Add the beans and cook for 10 minutes or until the vegetables are tender. Serve with rice.

PREPARATION TIME: 20 MINUTES   COOKING TIME: 50 MINUTES

Orange sweet potato and spinach stir-fry

SPANOKOPITA

1.5 kg (3 lb 5 oz) silverbeet (Swiss chard)
1 white onion
10 spring onions (scallions)
60 ml (2 fl oz/$^1/_4$ cup) olive oil
1$^1/_2$ tablespoons chopped dill
200 g (7 oz) Greek feta cheese, crumbled
125 g (4$^1/_2$ oz/$^1/_2$ cup) cottage cheese
35 g (1$^1/_4$ oz/$^1/_3$ cup) finely grated kefalotyri cheese (see Note)
$^1/_4$ teaspoon freshly grated nutmeg
4 eggs, lightly beaten
10 sheets filo pastry
80 g (2$^3/_4$ oz) butter, melted, to brush

SERVES 4–6

Rinse and drain the silverbeet thoroughly. Discard the stems and shred the leaves. Finely chop the onion. Chop the spring onions, including some green.

Heat the olive oil in a large frying pan, add the onion and cook, stirring, over medium heat for 5 minutes, or until softened. Add the spring onion and silverbeet and cook, covered, over medium heat for 5 minutes. Add the dill and cook, uncovered, for 3–4 minutes, or until most of the liquid has evaporated. Remove from the heat and cool to room temperature.

Preheat the oven to 180°C (350°F/Gas 4) and lightly grease a 20 x 25 cm (8 x 10 inch) 2.5 litre (88 fl oz/10 cup) ovenproof dish. Put the feta, cottage and kefalotyri in a large bowl. Stir in the silverbeet mixture and add the nutmeg. Gradually add the eggs and combine well. Season to taste.

Line the base and sides of the dish with a sheet of filo pastry — keep the rest covered with a damp tea towel (dish towel) to prevent them from drying out. Brush with some of the melted butter and cover with another sheet of pastry. Butter the sheet and repeat in this way, using five sheets of pastry. Spoon the filling into the dish and level the surface. Fold the exposed pastry up and over to cover the top of the filling. Cover with a sheet of pastry, brush with butter and continue until all the remaining sheets are used. Roughly trim the pastry with kitchen scissors then tuck the excess inside the wall of the dish.

Brush the top with butter. Using a sharp knife, score the surface into squares. Sprinkle a few drops of cold water on top to prevent the pastry from curling. Bake for 45 minutes, or until puffed and golden. Rest at room temperature for 10 minutes before serving.

PREPARATION TIME: 25 MINUTES +   COOKING TIME: 1 HOUR

NOTE: Kefalotyri is a Greek cheese made from 100% pasteurized sheep's milk. It is a hard pale golden-yellow cheese with a tangy flavour and sharp aroma. It is usually grated, like parmesan or pecorino. You can use pecorino if kefalotyri is unavailable.

ALMOND AND BROCCOLI STIR-FRY

1 teaspoon coriander seeds
500 g (1 lb 2 oz) broccoli
60 ml (2 fl oz/¼ cup) olive oil
2 tablespoons slivered almonds
1 garlic clove, crushed
1 teaspoon finely shredded fresh ginger
2 tablespoons red wine vinegar
1 tablespoon soy sauce
2 teaspoons sesame oil
1 teaspoon toasted sesame seeds (see Note)

SERVES 4

Lightly crush the coriander seeds using a mortar and pestle or with a rolling pin. Cut the broccoli into small florets.

Heat the oil in a wok or a large heavy-based frying pan and swirl to coat the base and side. Add the coriander seeds and almonds. Stir quickly over medium heat for 1 minute, or until the almonds are golden.

Add the garlic, ginger and broccoli to the pan. Stir-fry over high heat for 2 minutes. Remove the pan from the heat. Pour the combined vinegar, soy sauce and sesame oil into the pan. Toss until the broccoli is well coated. Serve immediately, sprinkled with toasted sesame seeds.

PREPARATION TIME: 10 MINUTES   COOKING TIME: 5 MINUTES

NOTE: Toast the sesame seeds in a dry frying pan over medium heat, stirring constantly, until they are lightly golden. Watch carefully as they will burn easily.

CAULIFLOWER, TOMATO AND GREEN PEA CURRY

1 small cauliflower
1 onion
2 large tomatoes
235 g (8½ oz/1½ cups) peas
60 ml (2 fl oz/¼ cup) ghee or oil
1 teaspoon crushed garlic
1 teaspoon grated fresh ginger
¾ teaspoon ground turmeric
1 tablespoon ground coriander
1 tablespoon ready-made vindaloo paste
2 teaspoons sugar
2 cardamom pods, lightly crushed
185 g (6½ oz/¾ cup) plain yoghurt

SERVES 4–6

Cut the cauliflower into small florets. Thinly slice the onion and cut the tomatoes into thin wedges. Steam the cauliflower and peas until tender.

Heat the ghee in a large saucepan and cook the onion, garlic and ginger over medium heat until soft and golden. Add the turmeric, coriander, vindaloo paste, sugar, cardamom pods and yoghurt and cook for 3–4 minutes. Add the tomato and cook for 3–4 minutes.

Add the cauliflower and peas and simmer for 3–4 minutes. Serve with rice.

PREPARATION TIME: 25 MINUTES   COOKING TIME: 20 MINUTES

Almond and broccoli stir-fry

SPICY CHICKPEA AND VEGETABLE CASSEROLE

335 g (11¾ oz/1½ cups) dried chickpeas (see Note)
1 large onion
300 g (10½ oz) pumpkin (winter squash)
150 g (5½ oz) green beans
200 g (7 oz) button squash
2 tablespoons oil
1 garlic clove, crushed
3 teaspoons ground cumin
½ teaspoon chilli powder
½ teaspoon ground allspice
425 g (15 oz) tinned peeled tomatoes, crushed
375 ml (13 fl oz/1½ cups) vegetable stock
2 tablespoons tomato paste (concentrated purée)
1 teaspoon dried oregano

SERVES 4

Put the chickpeas in a large bowl. Cover with cold water and soak overnight. Drain.

Chop the onion. Cut the pumpkin into large cubes. Top and tail the beans. Cut the button squash into quarters.

Heat the oil in a large saucepan. Add the onions and garlic and stir-fry for 2 minutes, or until tender. Add the cumin, chilli powder and allspice. Stir-fry for 1 minute. Add the chickpeas, tomatoes and vegetable stock to the pan. Bring to the boil, then reduce the heat and simmer, covered, for 1 hour, stirring occasionally.

Add the pumpkin, beans, squash, tomato paste and oregano. Stir to combine. Simmer, covered, for another 15 minutes. Remove the lid from the pan and simmer, uncovered, for another 10 minutes to reduce and slightly thicken the sauce.

PREPARATION TIME: 25 MINUTES +   COOKING TIME: 1 HOUR 30 MINUTES

NOTE: A quick way to soak chickpeas is to place them in a large saucepan and cover with cold water. Bring to the boil, then remove from the heat and soak for two hours. If you are in a hurry, substitute tinned chickpeas. Drain and rinse thoroughly before use.

POTATO CURRY WITH SESAME SEEDS

4 large potatoes
1 tablespoon oil
1 teaspoon cumin seeds
1 teaspoon coriander seeds
2 teaspoons mustard seeds
2 tablespoons sesame seeds
1/2 teaspoon turmeric
1 teaspoon chopped chilli
2 teaspoons finely grated lemon zest
2 tablespoons lemon juice

SERVES 4

Boil, steam or microwave the potatoes until tender. Leave to cool, then peel and chop them. Heat the oil in a large heavy-based frying pan over medium heat. Cook the cumin, coriander and mustard seeds for 1 minute, stirring constantly.

Add the sesame seeds and cook for 1–2 minutes, stirring until golden. Add the turmeric, chilli, potato, lemon zest and juice. Stir until well combined and heated through. Season to taste.

PREPARATION TIME: 20 MINUTES   COOKING TIME: 20 MINUTES

MEXICAN TOMATO BAKE

6 ripe tomatoes
2 red onions
1 green capsicum (pepper)
2 tablespoons oil
2 garlic cloves, crushed
1 tablespoon red wine vinegar
1 teaspoon sugar
1/2 teaspoon chilli powder
375 g (13 oz) tinned corn kernels, drained
125 g (4 1/2 oz) plain corn chips
150 g (5 1/2 oz/1 1/4 cups) grated cheddar cheese
250 g (9 oz/1 cup) sour cream
snipped chives, to garnish

SERVES 4–6

Score a cross in the base of each tomato. Put in a heatproof bowl and cover with boiling water. Leave for 30 seconds, then transfer to cold water, drain and peel away the skin from the cross. Cut the tomatoes in half, scoop out the seeds and chop the flesh. Chop the onion. Cut the capsicum in half, remove the seeds and membrane and chop. Preheat the oven to 160°C (315°F/Gas 2–3).

To make the sauce, heat the oil in a saucepan. Add the onions and garlic and cook over medium heat for 3 minutes. Add the tomato, capsicum, vinegar, sugar and chilli. Cook, uncovered, for 6–7 minutes, or until the tomato is soft and the liquid has evaporated. Stir in the corn kernels over heat for 3 minutes.

Arrange layers of corn chips, sauce and cheese in an ovenproof dish, finishing with a cheese layer.

Spread with the sour cream. Bake, uncovered, for 15 minutes. Sprinkle with chives before serving.

PREPARATION TIME: 25 MINUTES +   COOKING TIME: 30 MINUTES

Potato curry with sesame seeds

TOFU WITH CHILLI JAM AND CASHEWS

2 red capsicums (peppers)
80 ml (2¹/₂ fl oz/¹/₃ cup) peanut oil
12 red Asian shallots, chopped
8 garlic cloves, chopped
8 long red chillies, chopped
1 tablespoon tamarind purée
1 tablespoon soy sauce
100 g (3¹/₂ oz) palm sugar (jaggery) or soft brown sugar, grated
2 tablespoons kecap manis (see Notes)
6 spring onions (scallions)
750 g (1 lb 10 oz) silken firm tofu
1 tablespoon peanut oil, extra
25 g (³/₄ oz) Thai basil
100 g (3¹/₂ oz) roasted salted cashews

SERVES 4

To make the chilli jam, cut the capsicum in half, remove the seeds and membrane and chop. Heat half of the peanut oil in a frying pan. Add the shallots and garlic and cook over medium heat for 2 minutes. Transfer to a food processor, add the chilli and red capsicum and process until smooth. Heat the remaining oil in the pan, add the shallot mixture and cook over medium heat for 2 minutes. Stir in the tamarind, soy sauce and palm sugar and cook for 20 minutes.

To make the stir-fry sauce, combine 2–3 tablespoons of the chilli jam with the kecap manis in a small bowl.

Cut the spring onion into 3 cm (1¹/₄ inch) lengths and the tofu into 3 cm (1¹/₄ inch) cubes. Heat the extra peanut oil in a non-stick wok over high heat and swirl to coat the base and side. Add the spring onion and cook for 30 seconds. Remove. Add the tofu, stir-fry for 1 minute, then add the stir-fry sauce. Cook for 3 minutes, or until the tofu is coated and heated through. Return the spring onion to the wok, add the basil and cashews and cook until the basil has wilted.

PREPARATION TIME: 20 MINUTES   COOKING TIME: 30 MINUTES

NOTES: You can keep the rest of the chilli jam in a sterilized jar for up to 6 months.

Kecap manis is an Indonesian sweet soy sauce. If you are unable to find it, use soy sauce sweetened with a little soft brown sugar.

TEMPEH STIR-FRY

1 red chilli
4 spring onions (scallions)
300 g (10^1/$_2$ oz) tempeh
800 g (1 lb 12 oz) Chinese broccoli
(gai larn)
1 teaspoon sesame oil
1 tablespoon peanut oil
2 garlic cloves, crushed
1 tablespoon grated fresh ginger
500 g (1 lb 2 oz) baby bok choy
(pak choy) leaves
125 ml (4 fl oz/^{1}/$_2$ cup) vegetarian oyster
sauce (see Notes)
2 tablespoons rice vinegar
2 tablespoons coriander (cilantro) leaves
40 g (1^1/$_2$ oz/^{1}/$_4$ cup) toasted cashew nuts
(see Notes)

SERVES 4

Thinly slice the chilli. Slice the spring onions, diagonally. Cut the tempeh into 2 cm (^{3}/$_4$ inch) cubes. Chop the Chinese broccoli. Heat a wok over high heat, add the sesame and peanut oils and swirl to coat the base and side. Add the garlic, ginger, chilli and spring onion and cook for 1–2 minutes, or until the onion is soft. Add the tempeh to the wok and cook for 5 minutes, or until golden. Remove from the wok. Add half the greens and 1 tablespoon water to the wok and cook, covered, for 3–4 minutes, or until the greens have wilted. Remove from the wok and repeat with the remaining greens and a little more water. Return the greens and tempeh to the wok, add the vegetarian oyster sauce and vinegar and warm through. Top with the coriander and nuts. Serve with rice.

PREPARATION TIME: 15 MINUTES   COOKING TIME: 15 MINUTES

NOTES: Vegetarian oyster sauce is available from Asian food stores.
    Toast the cashew nuts in a dry frying pan over medium heat, stirring constantly, until they are golden brown and fragrant. Watch carefully as they will burn easily.

TOFU AND SNOW PEA STIR-FRY

600 g (1 lb 5 oz) firm tofu, drained
400 g (14 oz) fresh Asian mushrooms
(such as shiitake or oyster)
60 ml (2 fl oz/^{1}/$_4$ cup) peanut oil
2 teaspoons sambal oelek or chilli paste
(see Notes)
2 garlic cloves, finely chopped
300 g (10^1/$_2$ oz) snow peas (mangetout),
trimmed
60 ml (2 fl oz/^{1}/$_4$ cup) kecap manis
(see Notes)

SERVES 4

Cut the tofu into 2 cm (^{3}/$_4$ inch) cubes. Slice the mushrooms. Heat a wok over high heat, add 2 tablespoons of the peanut oil and swirl to coat the base and side of the wok. Add the tofu in two batches and stir-fry each batch for 2–3 minutes, or until lightly browned on all sides, then transfer to a plate. Heat the remaining oil in the wok, add the sambal oelek, garlic, snow peas, mushrooms and 1 tablespoon water and stir-fry for 1–2 minutes, or until the vegetables are almost cooked but still crunchy. Return the tofu to the wok, add the kecap manis and stir-fry for 1 minute, or until heated through. Serve immediately with steamed rice.

PREPARATION TIME: 10 MINUTES   COOKING TIME: 15 MINUTES

NOTES: Kecap manis is an Indonesian sweet soy sauce. If you are unable to find it, use soy sauce sweetened with a little soft brown sugar.
    Sambal oelek is a Southeast Asian chilli paste.

Tempeh stir-fry

LENTIL BHUJA CASSEROLE

375 g (13 oz/2 cups) green lentils
200 g (7 oz) green beans
2 carrots
1 large onion
1 large potato
1 teaspoon ground cumin
1 teaspoon ground coriander
1 teaspoon ground turmeric
90 g (3¼ oz/¾ cup) plain (all-purpose) flour
oil, for pan-frying
2 tablespoons oil, extra
2 garlic cloves, crushed
1 tablespoon grated fresh ginger
250 ml (9 fl oz/1 cup) tomato passata (puréed tomatoes)
500 ml (17 fl oz/2 cups) vegetable stock
250 ml (9 fl oz/1 cup) pouring (whipping) cream
pitta bread, to serve

SERVES 4–6

Cover the lentils with cold water and soak overnight. Drain well.

Top and tail the beans. Slice the carrots. Grate the onion and potato and drain the excess liquid. Combine the lentils, onion, potato, cumin, coriander, turmeric and flour in a bowl, and mix well. Roll the mixture into walnut-sized balls and place them on a foil-lined tray. Cover and refrigerate for 30 minutes.

Heat the oil, about 2 cm (¾ inch) deep, in a frying pan. Add the lentil balls in small batches and fry over high heat for 5 minutes, or until golden brown. Drain on paper towel.

Heat the extra oil in a large saucepan. Add the garlic and ginger and cook, stirring, over medium heat for 1 minute. Stir in the tomato purée, vegetable stock and cream. Bring to the boil, reduce the heat and simmer, uncovered, for 10 minutes. Add the lentil balls, beans and carrot, cover and simmer for 35 minutes, stirring occasionally. Serve with pitta bread.

PREPARATION TIME: 40 MINUTES +   COOKING TIME: 1 HOUR 10 MINUTES

NOTE: Make sure your hands are dry when shaping the lentil mixture into balls. The lentil balls can be made a day ahead and stored in an airtight container in the refrigerator.

GREEN CURRY WITH SWEET POTATO AND EGGPLANT

1 onion
1 eggplant (aubergine)
1 orange sweet potato
1 tablespoon vegetable oil
1-2 tablespoons green curry paste
(see Note)
375 ml (13 fl oz/1¹/2 cups) coconut milk
250 ml (9 fl oz/1 cup) vegetable stock
6 makrut (kaffir lime) leaves
2 teaspoons grated palm sugar (jaggery)
or soft brown sugar
2 tablespoons lime juice
2 teaspoons lime zest
coriander (cilantro) leaves, to garnish
makrut (kaffir lime) leaves, extra, to
garnish (optional)

SERVES 4-6

Chop the onion. Quarter and slice the eggplant and cut the sweet potato into cubes. Heat the oil in a large wok. Add the onion and green curry paste and cook, stirring, over medium heat for 3 minutes. Add the eggplant and cook for a further 4-5 minutes, or until softened. Pour in the coconut milk and vegetable stock, bring to the boil, then reduce the heat and simmer for 5 minutes. Add the makrut (kaffir lime) leaves and sweet potato and cook, stirring occasionally, for 10 minutes, or until the eggplant and sweet potato are very tender.

Mix in the sugar, lime juice and lime zest until well combined with the vegetables. Season to taste with salt. Garnish with some coriander leaves and extra makrut (kaffir lime) leaves if desired, and serve with steamed rice.

PREPARATION TIME: 15 MINUTES   COOKING TIME: 25 MINUTES

NOTE: Make sure you read the label and choose a green curry paste without shrimp paste.

DRY POTATO AND PEA CURRY

2 onions
750 g (1 lb 10 oz) potatoes
2 teaspoons brown mustard seeds
2 tablespoons ghee or oil
2 garlic cloves, crushed
2 teaspoons grated fresh ginger
1 teaspoon ground turmeric
¹/2 teaspoon chilli powder
1 teaspoon ground cumin
1 teaspoon garam masala
100 g (3¹/2 oz/²/3 cup) peas
2 tablespoons chopped mint

SERVES 4

Slice the onion and cut the potatoes into cubes. Put the mustard seeds in a large dry saucepan and cook over medium heat until the seeds start to pop. Add the ghee, onion, garlic and ginger, and cook, stirring, until the onion is soft.

Add the turmeric, chilli powder, cumin, garam masala and potato. Stir until the potato is coated. Add 125 ml (4 fl oz/¹/2 cup) water, cover and simmer for 15-20 minutes, or until the potato is just tender, stirring occasionally.

Add the peas and stir until combined. Season to taste. Simmer, covered, for 3-5 minutes, or until the potato is cooked through and the liquid is absorbed. Stir in the mint and serve with rice.

PREPARATION TIME: 15 MINUTES   COOKING TIME: 25 MINUTES

Green curry with sweet potato and eggplant

SWEET VEGETABLE CURRY

2 carrots
1 parsnip
1 potato
1 green capsicum (pepper)
2 onions
300 g (10$^1/_2$ oz) cauliflower
2 tablespoons oil
1 teaspoon ground cardamom
$^1/_4$ teaspoon ground cloves
1$^1/_2$ teaspoons cumin seeds
1 teaspoon ground coriander
1 teaspoon ground turmeric
1 teaspoon brown mustard seeds
$^1/_2$ teaspoon chilli powder
2 teaspoons grated fresh ginger
330 ml (11$^1/_4$ fl oz/1$^1/_3$ cups) vegetable stock
185 ml (6 fl oz/$^3/_4$ cup) apricot nectar
2 tablespoons fruit chutney
200 g (7 oz) small button mushrooms
25 g ($^3/_4$ oz/$^1/_4$ cup) ground almonds

SERVES 4

Cut the carrots, parsnip and potato into 2 cm ($^3/_4$ inch) pieces. Cut the green capsicum in half, remove the seeds and membrane and cut into 2 cm ($^3/_4$ inch) squares. Chop the onions and cut the cauliflower into small florets.

Heat the oil in a large heavy-based saucepan. Add the onion and cook over medium heat for 4 minutes, or until just soft. Add the cardamom, cloves, cumin seeds, coriander, turmeric, mustard seeds, chilli powder and ginger and cook, stirring, for 1 minute or until aromatic.

Add the carrot, parsnip, potato, vegetable stock, apricot nectar and fruit chutney to the pan. Cook, covered, over medium heat for 25 minutes, stirring occasionally.

Stir in the capsicum, mushrooms and cauliflower. Simmer for 10 minutes, or until the vegetables are tender. Stir in the ground almonds and serve with rice.

PREPARATION TIME: 20 MINUTES   COOKING TIME: 40 MINUTES

NOTE: Any vegetables can be used in this curry. For example, broccoli, zucchini (courgette), red capsicum (pepper) or orange sweet potato would be suitable.

HUNGARIAN CASSEROLE

1 red capsicum (pepper)
1 green capsicum (pepper)
1 onion
4 large potatoes
1 tablespoon olive oil
30 g (1 oz) butter
440 g (15½ oz) tinned chopped tomatoes
250 ml (9 fl oz/1 cup) vegetable stock
2 teaspoons caraway seeds
2 teaspoons paprika

CRISPY CROUTONS
4 slices white bread
250 ml (9 fl oz/1 cup) oil

SERVES 4–6

Cut the red and green capsicums in half, remove the seeds and membrane and roughly chop. Chop the onion. Cut the potatoes into large chunks. Heat the oil and butter in a large heavy-based frying pan and cook the potatoes over medium heat, turning regularly, until crisp on the edges.

Add the onion and red and green capsicum and cook for 5 minutes. Add the tomatoes with juice, vegetable stock, caraway seeds and paprika. Season to taste. Simmer, uncovered, for 10 minutes or until the potatoes are tender.

Meanwhile, to make the croutons, remove the crusts from the bread and cut the bread into small cubes. Heat the oil in a frying pan over medium heat. Cook the bread, turning often, for 2 minutes or until golden brown and crisp. Drain on paper towel. Serve the croutons with the casserole.

PREPARATION TIME: 30 MINUTES   COOKING TIME: 30 MINUTES

PINEAPPLE CURRY

1 pineapple, or 450 g (1 lb) tinned pineapple pieces, drained
2 spring onions (scallions)
1 teaspoon cardamom seeds
1 teaspoon coriander seeds
1 teaspoon cumin seeds
½ teaspoon whole cloves
2 tablespoons oil
2 teaspoons grated fresh ginger
4 candlenuts, roughly chopped
1 teaspoon sambal oelek (see Note)
1 tablespoon chopped mint

SERVES 4 AS PART OF A SHARED MEAL

Peel and halve the pineapple, remove the core, and cut the pineapple into 2 cm (¾ inch) chunks. Cut the spring onion into 2 cm (¾ inch) pieces.

Grind the cardamom seeds, coriander seeds, cumin seeds and cloves using a mortar and pestle.

Heat the oil in a frying pan. Add the spring onion, ginger, candlenuts and spice mixture, and stir-fry over low heat for 3 minutes.

Add 250 ml (9 fl oz/1 cup) water, sambal oelek, mint and pineapple and bring to the boil. Reduce the heat to low, cover and simmer for 10 minutes, or until the pineapple is tender but still holding its shape.

PREPARATION TIME: 20 MINUTES   COOKING TIME: 15 MINUTES

NOTE: Sambal oelek is a Southeast Asian chilli paste.

INDIAN DAL WITH PITTA TOASTS

310 g (11 oz/1¼ cups) red lentils
1 onion
2 tablespoons ghee (see Note)
2 garlic cloves, crushed
1 teaspoon grated fresh ginger
1 teaspoon ground turmeric
1 teaspoon garam masala

PITTA TOASTS
4 pitta bread rounds
2–3 tablespoons olive oil

SERVES 4–6

Put the lentils in a large bowl and cover with water. Remove any floating particles and drain the lentils well.

Finely chop the onion. Heat the ghee in a saucepan. Fry the onion for about 3 minutes, or until soft. Add the garlic, ginger and spices and cook, stirring, for 1 minute.

Add the lentils and 500 ml (17 fl oz/2 cups) water and bring to the boil. Lower the heat and simmer, stirring occasionally, for 15 minutes, or until all the water has been absorbed. Watch carefully towards the end of cooking time, as the mixture could burn on the bottom of the pan.

Transfer to a serving bowl and serve warm or at room temperature with pitta toasts or with naan or pitta bread.

To make the pitta toasts, preheat the oven to 180°C (350°F/Gas 4). Cut the pitta bread into wedges and brush lightly with the oil. Arrange on a baking tray and cook for 5–7 minutes, or until lightly browned and crisp.

PREPARATION TIME: 15 MINUTES   COOKING TIME: 20–25 MINUTES

NOTE: Oil may be used instead of the ghee if ghee is difficult to obtain. You can also make your own ghee — melt some butter, skim away the white froth on the surface and then pour the clear butter into another container, leaving the white residue behind.

THAI COCONUT VEGETABLES

1 red capsicum (pepper)
2 small onions
2 celery stalks
150 g (5½ oz) green beans
1 tablespoon oil
1 teaspoon ground cumin
150 g (5½ oz) cauliflower florets
185 g (6½ oz/1½ cups) grated pumpkin (winter squash)
250 ml (9 fl oz/1 cup) coconut milk
250 ml (9 fl oz/1 cup) vegetable stock
1 tablespoon sweet chilli sauce
1 tablespoon finely chopped coriander (cilantro)

SERVES 4–6

Cut the capsicum in half, remove the seeds and membrane and chop. Cut the onion into wedges. Slice the celery diagonally and top and tail the beans. Heat the oil in a frying pan or wok. Add the onion and cumin and stir-fry over medium heat for 2 minutes, or until the onion is golden.

Add the cauliflower and stir-fry over high heat for 2 minutes. Add the red capsicum, celery and pumpkin and stir-fry over high heat for 2 minutes, or until the vegetables have begun to soften.

Add the coconut milk, stock and chilli sauce and bring to boil. Reduce the heat and cook, uncovered, for 8 minutes, or until the vegetables are almost tender. Cut the beans in half and add them to the pan with the coriander. Cook for 2 minutes, or until the beans are just tender. Serve with steamed rice.

PREPARATION TIME: 15–20 MINUTES   COOKING TIME: 15 MINUTES

MUSHROOM LASAGNE

250 g (9 oz) packet instant lasagne sheets
310 g (11 oz/1¼ cups) ready-made pasta sauce
4 spring onions (scallions)
2 tablespoons oil
2 garlic cloves, crushed
500 g (1 lb 2 oz) button mushrooms
2 tablespoons chopped basil leaves
250 g (9 oz/1 cup) ricotta cheese, crumbled
50 g (1¾ oz/½ cup) freshly grated parmesan cheese
½ teaspoon ground nutmeg
155 g (5½ oz) rocket (arugula)
60 g (2¼ oz/½ cup) grated cheddar cheese
75 g (2¾ oz/½ cup) grated mozzarella cheese

SERVES 6

Preheat the oven to 200°C (400°F/Gas 6). Divide the lasagne sheets into three equal portions. Spread 60 g (2½ oz/¼ cup) of the pasta sauce into the base of a large, rectangular ovenproof dish. Top with a layer of lasagne sheets. Slice the spring onions.

Heat the oil in a frying pan, add the garlic and spring onion and cook for 3 minutes. Add the mushrooms and cook for 5 minutes. Remove from the heat and stir in the basil.

Spread half of the mushroom mixture in a layer on the pasta sheets, then top with half of the ricotta. Sprinkle with half of the parmesan, the nutmeg and the rocket. Layer the second portion of lasagne sheets on top, then half of the remaining pasta sauce.

Repeat the top layer with the remaining ingredients, finishing with pasta sauce. Scatter the cheddar and mozzarella over the top and bake for 40–50 minutes until the lasagne is tender and the topping is golden.

PREPARATION TIME: 20 MINUTES   COOKING TIME: 1 HOUR

Thai coconut vegetables

BORLOTTI BEAN MOUSSAKA

250 g (9 oz/1¼ cups) dried borlotti
(cranberry) beans
2 large eggplants (aubergines)
80 ml (2½ fl oz/⅓ cup) olive oil
1 onion
125 g (4½ oz) button mushrooms
1 garlic clove, crushed
2 x 440 g (15½ oz) tins peeled tomatoes,
chopped
250 ml (9 fl oz/1 cup) red wine
1 tablespoon tomato paste
(concentrated purée)
1 tablespoon chopped oregano

TOPPING
250 g (9 oz/1 cup) plain yoghurt
4 eggs, lightly beaten
500 ml (17 fl oz/2 cups) milk
¼ teaspoon paprika
50 g (1¾ oz/½ cup) freshly grated
parmesan cheese
40 g (1½ oz/½ cup) fresh breadcrumbs

SERVES 6

Soak the borlotti beans in cold water overnight. Rinse and drain well.

Put the borlotti beans in a large heavy-based saucepan, cover with water and bring to the boil. Reduce the heat and simmer for 1½ hours, or until tender. Drain the beans.

Meanwhile, slice the eggplant, sprinkle with salt and set aside for 30 minutes. Rinse and pat dry. Brush the eggplant slices with a little of the oil and cook under a preheated grill (broiler) for 3 minutes each side, or until golden. Drain on paper towel. Chop the onion and slice the mushrooms.

Preheat the oven to 200°C (400°F/Gas 6). Heat the remaining oil in a large heavy-based saucepan. Add the garlic and onion and cook over medium heat for 3 minutes, or until the onion is golden. Add the mushrooms and cook for 3 minutes, or until browned. Stir in the tomatoes, wine, tomato paste and oregano. Bring to the boil, reduce the heat and simmer for 40 minutes, or until the sauce has thickened.

To assemble the moussaka, spoon the borlotti beans into a large, ovenproof dish and top with tomato sauce and eggplant slices.

To make the topping, whisk together the yoghurt, eggs, milk and paprika. Pour over the eggplant and set aside for 10 minutes. Combine the parmesan cheese and breadcrumbs and sprinkle over the moussaka. Bake for 45–60 minutes, or until the moussaka is heated through and the top is golden.

PREPARATION TIME: 45 MINUTES +   COOKING TIME: 2 HOURS 30 MINUTES

CHINESE VEGETABLES WITH GINGER

4 spring onions (scallions)
235 g (8^1/$_2$ oz) tinned water chestnuts
1 tablespoon oil
3 teaspoons grated fresh ginger
425 g (15 oz) tinned baby corn, drained
45 g (1^3/$_4$ oz/1 cup) finely shredded Chinese cabbage (wong bok)
125 g (4^1/$_2$ oz) bean sprouts, trimmed
1 tablespoon soy sauce
1–2 tablespoons vegetarian oyster sauce (see Note)
2 teaspoons sesame oil

SERVES 4

Slice the spring onions and water chestnuts. Heat the oil in a heavy-based frying pan or wok and add the ginger and spring onion. Stir-fry over high heat for 1 minute. Add the water chestnuts and baby corn and stir-fry for 30 seconds.

Add the Chinese cabbage, bean sprouts and soy and vegetarian oyster sauces and stir-fry for 1 minute. Stir in the sesame oil and toss well. Serve immediately.

PREPARATION TIME: 10–15 MINUTES   COOKING TIME: 5 MINUTES

NOTE: Vegetarian oyster sauce is available from Asian food stores.

CAULIFLOWER AND PASTA BAKE WITH CROUTON TOPPING

600 g (1 lb 5 oz) cauliflower
2 red onions
150 g (5^1/$_2$ oz) short pasta (such as penne)
2 tablespoons olive oil
2 garlic cloves, finely chopped
80 g (2^3/$_4$ oz) butter
40 g (1^1/$_2$ oz/^{1}/$_3$ cup) plain (all-purpose) flour
1 litre (35 fl oz/4 cups) milk
200 g (7 oz/2 cups) freshly grated parmesan cheese
30 g (1 oz) shredded basil
5 slices day-old bread
50 g (1^3/$_4$ oz) butter, melted

SERVES 6

Cut the cauliflower into florets and chop the onion. Preheat the oven to 180°C (350°F/Gas 4). Cook the pasta in a saucepan of rapidly boiling salted water until *al dente*. Drain. Steam the cauliflower until just tender. Heat the olive oil in a frying pan. Fry the onion and garlic over medium heat until the onions are soft. Combine with the cauliflower.

Melt the butter in a large saucepan. Blend in the flour and cook, stirring constantly, for 1 minute. Gradually whisk in the milk. Stir constantly until the mixture boils and thickens. Remove from the heat and stir through the basil and 125 g (4^1/$_2$ oz/1^1/$_4$ cups) of the parmesan. Add the cauliflower, pasta and onion to the sauce and mix thoroughly.

Spoon the cauliflower mix into a large ovenproof dish. Remove the crusts from the bread and cut the bread into large cubes. Toss the cubes in the melted butter and then scatter them over the cauliflower mixture. Sprinkle with the remaining parmesan. Bake for 35–40 minutes until the top is golden.

PREPARATION TIME: 25 MINUTES   COOKING TIME: 1 HOUR

Chinese vegetables with ginger

INDONESIAN PUMPKIN AND SPINACH CURRY

CURRY PASTE
3 candlenuts
1 tablespoon peanuts
2 red Asian shallots
2 garlic cloves
2–3 teaspoons sambal oelek (see Note)
1/4 teaspoon ground turmeric
1 teaspoon grated fresh galangal

1 onion
600 g (1 lb 5 oz) butternut pumpkin (squash)
350 g (12 oz) English spinach
2 tablespoons vegetable oil
250 ml (9 fl oz/1 cup) vegetable stock
400 ml (14 fl oz) coconut cream
1/4 teaspoon sugar

SERVES 4

To make the curry paste, combine all the ingredients in a food processor or blender and process to a smooth paste.

Finely chop the onion. Cut the butternut pumpkin into 2 cm (3/4 inch) cubes and roughly chop the English spinach.

Heat a wok over high heat, add the oil and swirl to coat the base and side. Add the curry paste and cook, stirring, over low heat for 3–5 minutes, or until fragrant. Add the onion and cook for 5 minutes.

Add the pumpkin and half the stock and cook, covered, for 10 minutes, or until the pumpkin is almost cooked through. Pour in more stock, if required. Add the spinach, coconut cream and sugar, and season with salt. Bring to the boil, stirring constantly, then reduce the heat and simmer for 3–5 minutes, or until the spinach is cooked and the sauce has thickened slightly.

PREPARATION TIME: 20 MINUTES   COOKING TIME: 25 MINUTES

NOTE: Sambal oelek is a Southeast Asian chilli paste.

SPICY EGGS AND SNAKE BEANS

4 spring onions (scallions)
300 g (10½ oz) snake (yard-long) beans
1 teaspoon sesame oil
1 tablespoon oil
2 garlic cloves, crushed
200 g (7 oz) mixed mushrooms
(see Notes)
8 eggs, lightly beaten
1 tablespoon kecap manis (see Notes)
2 teaspoons sambal oelek (see Notes)
3 tablespoons chopped mint
3 tablespoons chopped coriander
(cilantro) leaves

SERVES 4

Chop the spring onions and cut the snake beans into 5 cm (2 inch) lengths. Heat the combined oils in a wok or large frying pan, add the garlic and spring onion and cook over moderately high heat for 2 minutes.

Add the beans and mushrooms and stir-fry for 1 minute. Remove from the wok. Add the combined eggs, kecap manis, sambal oelek, mint and coriander to the centre of the wok. Allow to set for 2 minutes.

Return the vegetables to the wok and stir-fry, breaking up the egg, for 2 minutes or until the mixture is heated through. Serve with steamed rice.

PREPARATION TIME: 20 MINUTES   COOKING TIME: 15 MINUTES

NOTES: Use any combination of mushrooms up to the weight given. Some suitable mushrooms are button, oyster, shiitake or enoki.

Kecap manis is an Indonesian sweet soy sauce. If you are unable to find it, use soy sauce sweetened with a little soft brown sugar. Sambal oelek is a Southeast Asian chilli paste.

VEGETABLE COCONUT CURRY

300 g (10½ oz) pumpkin (winter squash)
200 g (7 oz) potato
250 g (9 oz) okra
1 onion
2 tablespoons oil
1 garlic clove, crushed
3 green chillies, seeded and very finely chopped
½ teaspoon ground turmeric
½ teaspoon fenugreek seeds
8 curry leaves
1 cinnamon stick
500 ml (17 fl oz/2 cups) coconut milk

SERVES 4 AS PART OF A SHARED MEAL

Cut the pumpkin into 2 cm (¾ inch) cubes. Cut the potato into 2 cm (¾ inch) cubes. Trim the stems from the okra. Chop the onion.

Heat the oil in a large heavy-based saucepan. Add the garlic, chilli, turmeric, fenugreek seeds and onion, and cook over medium heat for 5 minutes, or until the onion is soft.

Add the pumpkin, potato, okra, curry leaves, cinnamon stick and coconut milk. Bring to the boil, then reduce the heat and simmer, uncovered, for 25–30 minutes, or until the vegetables are tender. Serve with rice.

PREPARATION TIME: 40 MINUTES   COOKING TIME: 30 MINUTES

Spicy eggs and snake beans

TOFU IN BLACK BEAN SAUCE

1 red capsicum (pepper)
450 g (1 lb) firm tofu
300 g (10½ oz) baby bok choy (pak choy)
50 g (1¾ oz/¼ cup) black beans, rinsed
4 spring onions (scallions)
80 ml (2½ fl oz/⅓ cup) vegetable stock
2 teaspoons cornflour (cornstarch)
2 teaspoons Chinese rice wine
1 teaspoon sesame oil
1 tablespoon soy sauce
2 tablespoons peanut oil
2 garlic cloves, very finely chopped
2 teaspoons finely chopped fresh ginger

SERVES 4

Cut the red capsicum in half, remove the seeds and membrane and cut into 2 cm (¾ inch) chunks. Cut the tofu into 2 cm (¾ inch) cubes and chop the baby bok choy, crossways, into 2 cm (¾ inch) pieces. Finely chop the black beans and slice the spring onions, diagonally, including some green.

Combine the vegetable stock, cornflour, Chinese rice wine, sesame oil, soy sauce, ½ teaspoon salt and some freshly ground black pepper.

Heat a wok over medium heat, add the peanut oil and swirl to coat the base and side. Add the tofu and stir-fry in two batches for 3 minutes each batch, or until lightly browned. Remove with a slotted spoon and drain on paper towel. Discard any bits of tofu stuck to the wok or floating in the oil.

Add the garlic and ginger and stir-fry for 30 seconds. Toss in the black beans and spring onion and stir-fry for 30 seconds. Add the red capsicum and stir-fry for 1 minute. Add the bok choy and stir-fry for 2 minutes. Return the tofu to the wok and stir gently. Pour in the sauce and stir gently for 2–3 minutes, or until the sauce has thickened slightly. Serve immediately with steamed rice.

PREPARATION TIME: 20 MINUTES   COOKING TIME: 15 MINUTES

239

WINTER VEGETABLE CASSEROLE

200 g (7 oz) pumpkin (winter squash)
2 potatoes
1 parsnip
30 g (1 oz) butter
1 tablespoon plain (all-purpose) flour
375 ml (13 fl oz/1½ cups) milk
½ teaspoon ground nutmeg
cress, to garnish

CRUMBLE TOPPING
80 g (2¾ oz/1 cup) fresh breadcrumbs
100 g (3½ oz) roasted cashew nuts,
roughly chopped
30 g (1 oz) butter

SERVES 4

Cut the pumpkin into large bite-sized pieces and cut the potato and parsnip into smaller pieces. Cook the vegetables in a large saucepan of boiling water for 8 minutes, or until just tender. Drain, then arrange the cooked vegetables in the base of a large, deep ovenproof dish.

Melt the butter in a saucepan over low heat. Add the flour and cook, stirring constantly, for 1 minute. Remove from the heat and gradually stir in the milk. Return the pan to the heat and bring the mixture to the boil, stirring constantly, until thickened. Boil for 1 minute. Add the nutmeg and season to taste. Pour the sauce over the vegetables. Preheat the oven to 180°C (350°F/Gas 4).

To make the crumble topping, combine the breadcrumbs and cashews. Sprinkle them over the vegetables. Dot the crumble topping with butter and bake for 30 minutes, or until golden. Garnish with cress, if desired.

PREPARATION TIME: 15 MINUTES   COOKING TIME: 40 MINUTES

STIR-FRIED ASPARAGUS WITH SESAME SEEDS

750 g (1 lb 10 oz) asparagus, trimmed
1 tablespoon sesame seeds
2 tablespoons oil
1 garlic clove, finely chopped
1 teaspoon grated fresh ginger
½ teaspoon sugar
2 teaspoons sesame oil
1 tablespoon soy sauce

SERVES 4

Cut the asparagus into 5 cm (2 inch) pieces.

Heat a wok or frying pan. Add the sesame seeds and stir-fry over high heat for 2 minutes, or until golden. Remove from the wok and set aside.

Heat the oil in the wok and add the garlic, ginger and asparagus. Stir-fry over high heat for 3 minutes, or until almost tender. Sprinkle the vegetables with ½ teaspoon pepper and add the sugar. Stir-fry over high heat for 1 minute.

Sprinkle with the sesame oil, soy sauce and sesame seeds and serve.

PREPARATION TIME: 10 MINUTES   COOKING TIME: 6 MINUTES

Winter vegetable casserole

SPINACH AND RICOTTA CANNELLONI

1 large onion
1 kg (2 lb 4 oz) English spinach
375 g (13 oz) fresh lasagne sheets
2 tablespoons olive oil
1–2 garlic cloves, crushed
650 g (1 lb 7 oz) ricotta cheese, beaten
2 eggs, beaten
1/4 teaspoon freshly grated nutmeg

TOMATO SAUCE
1 onion
500 g (1 lb 2 oz) very ripe tomatoes
1 tablespoon olive oil
2 garlic cloves, finely chopped
2 tablespoons tomato paste (concentrated purée)
1 teaspoon soft brown sugar
150 g (5 1/2 oz/1 cup) grated mozzarella cheese

SERVES 6

Finely chop the onion and English spinach. Cut the lasagne sheets into 15 even-sized pieces and trim lengthways so that they will fit neatly into a deep-sided, rectangular ovenproof dish when filled. Bring a large saucepan of water to a rapid boil and cook 1–2 lasagne sheets at a time until just softened. The amount of time will differ, depending on the type and brand of lasagne, but is usually about 2 minutes. Remove the sheets carefully with a wide strainer or sieve and lay out flat on a clean, damp tea towel (dish towel). Return the water to the boil and repeat the process with the remaining pasta sheets.

Heat the oil in a heavy-based frying pan. Cook the onion and garlic until golden, stirring regularly. Add the washed spinach, cook for 2 minutes, cover with a tight-fitting lid and steam for 5 minutes. Drain, removing as much liquid as possible. The spinach must be quite dry or the pasta will be soggy. Combine the spinach with the ricotta, eggs, nutmeg and season to taste. Mix well and set aside.

To make the tomato sauce, chop the onion and tomatoes. Heat the oil in a frying pan and cook the onion and garlic for 10 minutes over low heat, stirring occasionally. Add the tomato including the juice, the tomato paste, sugar, 125 ml (4 fl oz/1/2 cup) water and season. Bring the sauce to the boil, reduce the heat and simmer for 10 minutes. If a smoother sauce is preferred, purée in a food processor until the desired consistency is reached.

Preheat the oven to 180°C (350°F/Gas 4). Lightly brush the ovenproof dish with melted butter or oil. Spread about one-third of the tomato sauce over the base of the dish. Working with one piece of lasagne at a time, spoon 2 1/2 tablespoons of the spinach mixture down the centre of the sheet, leaving a border at each end. Roll up and lay, seam side down, in the dish. Repeat with the remaining pasta and filling. Spoon the remaining tomato sauce over the cannelloni and scatter the mozzarella over the top.

Bake for 30–35 minutes, or until golden brown and bubbling. Set aside for 10 minutes before serving. Garnish with fresh herb sprigs if desired.

PREPARATION TIME: 1 HOUR   COOKING TIME: 1 HOUR 15 MINUTES

NOTE: Dried cannelloni tubes can be used instead of lasagne sheets.

POTATO CAKE

8 roasting potatoes
30 g (1 oz) butter
2 tablespoons olive oil
1 garlic clove, crushed
200 g (7 oz/2 cups) dried breadcrumbs
125 g (4½ oz/1 cup) grated cheddar cheese
50 g (1¾ oz/½ cup) freshly grated parmesan cheese

Preheat the oven to 180°C (350°F/Gas 4). Brush a deep 20 cm (8 inch) spring-form tin with some melted butter. Line the base and side with baking paper.

Thinly slice the potato. Heat the butter and oil, then add the garlic and ½ teaspoon ground pepper. Overlap some potato slices in the base of the tin. Brush with the butter mixture. Sprinkle with some of the combined breadcrumbs and cheeses. Continue layering, ending with a layer of cheese. Press down firmly. Bake for 1 hour.

SERVES 4–6   PREPARATION TIME: 20 MINUTES   COOKING TIME: 1 HOUR 5 MINUTES

PASTA AND SPINACH TIMBALES

1 onion
30 g (1 oz) butter
1 tablespoon olive oil
500 g (1 lb 2 oz) English spinach, steamed and well-drained
8 eggs, lightly beaten
250 ml (9 oz/1 cup) pouring (whipping) cream
100 g (3½ oz) spaghetti or taglioni, cooked
60 g (2¼ oz/½ cup) grated cheddar cheese
50 g (1¾ oz/½ cup) freshly grated parmesan cheese

Chop the onion. Preheat the oven to 180°C (350°F/Gas 4). Brush six 250 ml (9 oz/1 cup) ramekins or dariole moulds with some melted butter or oil. Line the bases with baking paper. Heat the butter and oil together in a frying pan. Add the onion and stir over low heat until the onion is tender. Add the well-drained spinach and cook for 1 minute. Remove from the heat and leave to cool. Whisk in the eggs and cream. Stir in the spaghetti and grated cheeses then season to taste. Stir well and spoon into the prepared ramekins.

Place the ramekins in an ovenproof dish. Pour boiling water into the dish to come halfway up the sides of the ramekins. Bake for 30–35 minutes, or until set. Halfway through cooking you may need to cover the top with foil to prevent excess browning. Near the end of cooking time, test the timbales with the point of a knife. When cooked, the knife should come out clean.

SERVES 6   Allow the timbales to rest for 15 minutes before turning them out. Run the point of a knife around the edge of each ramekin. Invert onto serving plates.

PREPARATION TIME: 25 MINUTES   COOKING TIME: 45 MINUTES +

MUSHROOM NUT ROAST WITH TOMATO SAUCE

1 large onion
300 g (10¹/₂ oz) cap mushrooms
2 tablespoons olive oil
2 garlic cloves, crushed
200 g (7 oz) cashew nuts
200 g (7 oz) brazil nuts
125 g (4¹/₂ oz/1 cup) grated cheddar
cheese
25 g (³/₄ oz/¹/₄ cup) freshly grated
parmesan cheese
1 egg, lightly beaten
2 tablespoons snipped chives
80 g (2³/₄ oz/1 cup) fresh wholemeal
(whole-wheat) breadcrumbs
chives, extra, to garnish

TOMATO SAUCE
1 onion
1¹/₂ tablespoons olive oil
1 garlic clove, crushed
400 g (14 oz) tinned chopped tomatoes
1 tablespoon tomato paste (concentrated
purée)
1 teaspoon caster (superfine) sugar

SERVES 6

Grease a 14 x 21 cm (5¹/₂ x 8¹/₄ inch) loaf (bar) tin and line the base with baking paper.

Dice the onion and finely chop the mushrooms. Heat the oil in a frying pan and add the onion, garlic and mushrooms. Fry until soft, then cool.

Process the nuts in a food processor until finely chopped, but do not overprocess. Preheat the oven to 180°C (350°F/Gas 4).

Combine the cooled mushroom mixture, chopped nuts, cheddar, parmesan, egg, chives and breadcrumbs in a bowl. Mix well and season to taste. Press into the loaf tin and bake for 45 minutes, or until firm. Leave for 5 minutes, then turn out and garnish with the extra chives. Cut into slices to serve.

Meanwhile, to make the tomato sauce, finely chop the onion. Heat the oil in a saucepan, add the onion and garlic and cook, stirring frequently, for 5 minutes, or until soft but not brown. Stir in the tomato, tomato paste, sugar and 80 ml (2¹/₂ fl oz/¹/₃ cup) water. Simmer gently for 3–5 minutes, or until slightly thickened. Season. Serve the tomato sauce with the sliced nut roast.

PREPARATION TIME: 30 MINUTES   COOKING TIME: 1 HOUR

NOTE: For a variation, use a different mixture of nuts and add some seeds. You can use nuts such as pecans, almonds, hazelnuts (without skins) and pine nuts. Suitable seeds to use include sesame, pumpkin or sunflower seeds.

POTATO AND ZUCCHINI CASSEROLE

1 kg (2 lb 4 oz) ripe tomatoes
1 large red capsicum (pepper)
400 g (14 oz) small roasting potatoes, unpeeled
2 onions
400 g (14 oz) zucchini (courgettes)
60 ml (2¼ fl oz/¼ cup) olive oil
2 garlic cloves, crushed
1 teaspoon dried oregano
2 tablespoons chopped flat-leaf (Italian) parsley
2 tablespoons chopped dill
½ teaspoon ground cinnamon

SERVES 4–6

Preheat the oven to 180°C (350°F/Gas 4). Score a cross in the base of each tomato. Put in a heatproof bowl and cover with boiling water. Leave for 30 seconds, then transfer to cold water, drain and peel away the skin from the cross. Cut the tomatoes in half, scoop out the seeds and roughly chop the flesh. Cut the capsicum in half, remove the seeds and membrane from the red capsicum and cut the flesh into squares. Cut the potatoes into 1 cm (½ inch) slices. Slice the onion and thickly slice the zucchini.

Heat 2 tablespoons of the olive oil in a heavy-based frying pan over medium heat. Add the onion and cook, stirring frequently, for 10 minutes. Add the garlic and cook for 2 minutes. Put all the other ingredients in a large bowl and season generously. Add the softened onion and garlic and toss everything together. Transfer to a large ovenproof dish and drizzle the remaining oil over the vegetables.

Cover and bake for 1–1½ hours, or until the vegetables are tender, stirring every 30 minutes. Insert the point of a small knife into the potatoes. When the knife comes away easily, the potato is cooked.

PREPARATION TIME: 20 MINUTES   COOKING TIME: 1 HOUR 45 MINUTES

LAYERED POTATO AND APPLE BAKE

2 large all-purpose potatoes
3 green apples
1 onion
60 g (2¼ oz/½ cup) finely grated cheddar cheese
250 ml (9 fl oz/1 cup) pouring (whipping) cream
¼ teaspoon freshly ground nutmeg

SERVES 4–6

Preheat the oven to 180°C (350°F/Gas 4). Brush a large shallow ovenproof dish with melted butter or oil. Cut the potatoes into thin slices. Peel, core and quarter the apples, then cut them into thin slices. Slice the onion into very fine rings.

Layer the potatoes, apples and onion in the prepared dish, ending with a layer of potatoes. Sprinkle evenly with the cheddar. Pour the cream over the top, covering as evenly as possible. Sprinkle with the nutmeg and some black pepper to taste. Bake for 45 minutes, or until golden brown. Remove from the oven and allow to stand for 5 minutes before serving.

PREPARATION TIME: 30 MINUTES   COOKING TIME: 45 MINUTES

Potato and zucchini casserole

INDEX

INDEX

A

Algerian eggplant jam 101
almond and broccoli stir-fry 209
Andalusian asparagus 110
artichokes
    braised, with broad beans 97
    with tarragon mayonnaise 21
Asian greens with teriyaki tofu
    dressing 201
Asian mushroom risotto 142
asparagus
    Andalusian asparagus 110
    asparagus with sesame seeds 241
    tagliatelle with asparagus and
        herbs 141
aubergine see eggplant
avocado
    avocado with lime and chillies 61
    avocado salsa 81
    pumpkin with chilli and avocado 94
    spinach and avocado salad with
        warm mustard vinaigrette 85

B

beans
    beans with tomatoes 117
    borlotti bean moussaka 230
    braised artichokes with broad
        beans 97
    fettucine with creamy mushroom
        and bean sauce 178
    green beans in sesame seed sauce
        109
    Jamaican rice with peas 133
    lentil bhuja casserole 218
    lima bean casserole 193
    nachos with guacamole 57
    noodles in black bean sauce 145
    spicy eggs and snake beans 237
    spinach and nut salad 77
    tofu in black bean sauce 238
    vegetable donburi 182
beetroot hummus 49

bhel puri 14
black olive and capsicum tapenade 45
blue cheese tagliatelle 177
bondas 10
borlotti bean moussaka 230
broccoli
    almond and broccoli stir-fry 209
    tempeh stir-fry 217
bucatini with gorgonzola sauce 181
Buddhist vegetarian noodles 134

C

candied pumpkin 113
capsicums
    black olive and capsicum tapenade 45
    eggplant and capsicum grill 41
    Hungarian casserole 225
    linguine with red capsicum 157
    linguine with roasted vegetable
        sauce 137
    tofu with chilli jam and cashews 214
    vegetable lasagne 198
carrots
    spiced carrot and feta gnocchi 122
    Tunisian carrot salad 73
cashew nuts
    cashew nut curry 197
    chilli cashew noodles 186
    green pilaff with cashews 137
    potato and cashew samosas 41
    tofu with chilli jam and cashews 214
cauliflower
    cauliflower fritters 49
    cauliflower and pasta bake with
        crouton topping 233
    cauliflower, tomato and green pea
        curry 209
    vegetable korma 205
celery, spring onion and celery
    bundles 106
cheese
    baked ricotta 65
    blue cheese tagliatelle 177
    bucatini with gorgonzola sauce 181
    crispy cheese and curry lentil balls
        37

    curly endive and blue cheese salad
        89
    herbed cheese crackers 46
    herbed feta salad 73
    olive basil cheese spread 25
    potato baskets with cheese 65
    ricotta and basil with tagliatelle 153
    ricotta-filled ravioli with fresh
        tomato sauce 162
    rigatoni with tomato, haloumi and
        spinach 161
    spanokopita 206
    spiced carrot and feta gnocchi 122
    spinach and ricotta cannelloni 242
    spinach and ricotta gnocchi 153
    sweet potato rosti 114
    tomato and cheese risotto cakes
        170
chickpeas
    beetroot hummus 49
    chickpea chips 17
    chickpea curry 197
    chickpea and olive salad 81
    fried chickpeas 13
    lentil and chickpea burgers with
        coriander garlic cream 50
    spicy chickpea and vegetable
        casserole 210
chilli
    avocado with lime and chillies 61
    chilli cashew noodles 186
    chilli puffs with curried vegetables
        62
    chilli satay noodles 133
    chilli sauce 61
    marinated chilli mushrooms 17
    onion bhaji 57
    polenta chillies 33
    pumpkin with chilli and avocado 94
    spicy eggplant slices 109
    tempeh stir-fry 217
    tofu with chilli jam and cashews 214
    vegetarian phad thai 130
Chinese vegetables with ginger 233
coriander garlic cream 50
corn, spiced 105

corn and potato fritters 37
courgettes see zucchini
crispy cheese and curry lentil balls 37
curry
    cashew nut curry 197
    cauliflower, tomato and green pea
        209
    chickpea curry 197
    chilli puffs with curried vegetables
        62
    crispy cheese and curry lentil balls
        37
    dry potato and pea curry 221
    green curry with sweet potato and
        eggplant 221
    Indonesian pumpkin and spinach
        curry 234
    pea, egg and ricotta curry 194
    pineapple curry 225
    potato curry with sesame seeds 213
    pumpkin curry 193
    sweet vegetable curry 222
    vegetable coconut curry 237

D
dates
    lemon and date ziti 169
    orange and date salad 85
dip, marinated roasted vegetables 26
dolmades, vegetarian 66

E
eggplant
    Algerian eggplant jam 101
    borlotti bean moussaka 230
    chilli satay noodles 133
    eggplant and capsicum grill 41
    fettucine with green olives and
        eggplant 173
    green curry with sweet potato and
        eggplant 221
    ratatouille 98
    spicy eggplant slices 109
    sweet garlic eggplant 102
    tortellini with eggplant 129
    vegetable donburi 182

vegetable korma 205
vegetable lasagne 198
vegetarian sticky rice pockets 34
eggs
    egg fried rice 149
    pea, egg and ricotta curry 194
    spicy eggs and snake beans 237
endive, curly endive and blue cheese
    salad 89

F
fettucine
    with creamy mushroom and bean
        sauce 178
    with green olives and eggplant 173
    with zucchini and crisp-fried basil 177
fusilli with sage and garlic 145

G
garlic
    fusilli with sage and garlic 145
    garlic croutons 90
    garlic herb butter 154
    garlic mayonnaise 22
    lentil and chickpea burgers with
        coriander garlic cream 50
    pesto 53
    sweet garlic eggplant 102
guacamole 57

H
hazelnut pesto 21
herbs
    fettucine with zucchini and crisp-
        fried basil 177
    fusilli with sage and garlic 145
    herbed cheese crackers 46
    herbed feta salad 73
    mushrooms with herb nut butter 42
    noodles with vegetables and herbs
        173
    olive basil cheese spread 25
    potato and herb fritters 45
    potato and sage chips 25
    pumpkin gnocchi with sage butter
        138

ravioli with herbs 169
ricotta and basil with tagliatelle
    153
sautéed rosemary potatoes 105
spaghetti with herbs and tomato
    125
tagliatelle with asparagus and
    herbs 141
wild rice, thyme and mixed
    mushroom pilaff 126
Hungarian casserole 225

I
idlis 29
Indian dal with pitta toasts 226
Indonesian coconut and spice rice
    146
Indonesian pumpkin and spinach curry
    234

J
Jamaican rice with peas 133

K
khichhari 165
Korean pickled bean sprouts 93

L
leeks in white sauce 113
lemon and date ziti 169
lentils
    brown rice and puy lentils with
        pine nuts and spinach 181
    crispy cheese and curry lentil balls
        37
    Indian dal with pitta toasts 226
    khichhari 165
    lentil bhuja casserole 218
    lentil and chickpea burgers with
        coriander garlic cream 50
    Mediterranean lentil salad 86
    warm lentil and rice salad 70
lima bean casserole 193
linguine with red capsicum 157
    linguine with roasted vegetable
        sauce 137

M
Mediterranean lentil salad 86
Mexican tomato bake 213
mint chutney 14
minted cream sauce 122
mushrooms
    Asian mushroom risotto 142
    fettucine with creamy mushroom
        and bean sauce 178
    marinated chilli mushrooms 17
    mushroom lasagne 229
    mushroom nut roast with tomato
        sauce 246
    mushroom risotto fritters 185
    mushrooms with herb nut butter 42
    Oriental mushrooms with hokkein
        noodles 150
    pirozhki 54
    wild rice, thyme and mixed
        mushroom pilaff 126

N
nachos with guacamole 57
noodles
    Buddhist vegetarian noodles 134
    chilli cashew noodles 186
    chilli satay noodles 133
    noodles in black bean sauce 145
    noodles with vegetables and herbs
        173
    Oriental mushrooms with hokkein
        noodles 150
    potato noodles with vegetables 158
    tofu, peanut and noodle stir-fry 125
    udon noodle stir-fry 157
    vegetarian phad thai 130
nuts
    crunchy stuffed tofu puffs 61
    green olive, walnut and
        pomegranate salad 77
    Indonesian coconut and spice rice 146
    mushroom nut roast with tomato
        sauce 246
    mushrooms with herb nut butter 42
    penne with olive and pistachio
        pesto 129

pumpkin and pine nut tagliatelle
    149
spinach and nut salad 77
spinach with raisins and pine nuts
    117
Thai coconut vegetables 229
tofu, peanut and noodle stir-fry 125
vegetable coconut curry 237
see also cashew nuts

O
okra with coriander and tomato sauce
    97
olives
    black olive and capsicum tapenade
        45
    chickpea and olive salad 81
    fettucine with green olives and
        eggplant 173
    green olive, walnut and
        pomegranate salad 77
    olive basil cheese spread 25
    penne with olive and pistachio
        pesto 129
onions
    linguine with roasted vegetable
        sauce 137
    onion bhaji 57
    onion and parmesan pilaff 185
    spanokopita 206
    spring onion and celery bundles
        106
    sweet and sour onions 93
orange and date salad 85
orange sweet potato and spinach
    stir-fry 205

P
parmesan and pesto toasts 53
parsnip gnocchi 154
pasta
    blue cheese tagliatelle 177
    bucatini with gorgonzola sauce
        181
    cauliflower and pasta bake with
        crouton topping 233

fettucine with creamy mushroom
    and bean sauce 178
fettucine with green olives and
    eggplant 173
fettucine with zucchini and crisp-
    fried basil 177
fusilli with sage and garlic 145
lemon and date ziti 169
linguine with red capsicum 157
linguine with roasted vegetable
    sauce 137
pasta and spinach timbales 245
penne with olive and pistachio
    pesto 129
penne with rocket 141
pumpkin and pine nut tagliatelle
    149
ricotta and basil with tagliatelle 153
rigatoni with tomato, haloumi and
    spinach 161
spaghetti with herbs and tomato
    125
spinach and ricotta cannelloni 242
tagliatelle with asparagus and
    herbs 141
tortellini with eggplant 129
pears, sprout and pear salad with
    sesame dressing 74
peas
    cauliflower, tomato and green pea
        curry 209
    dry potato and pea curry 221
    pea, egg and ricotta curry 194
penne with olive and pistachio pesto
    129
penne with rocket 141
pesto 53
phad thai, vegetarian 130
pineapple curry 225
pirozhki 54
podi 29
polenta, baked, with spicy relish 38
polenta chillies 33
potatoes
    bondas 10
    corn and potato fritters 37

dry potato and pea curry 221

Hungarian casserole 225

layered potato and apple bake 249

potato baskets with cheese 65

potato cake 245

potato and cashew samosas 41

potato curry with sesame seeds 213

potato and herb fritters 45

potato and oil purée 101

potato and sage chips 25

potato and zucchini casserole 249

sautéed rosemary potatoes 105

pulao 174

pumpkin

candied pumpkin 113

Indonesian pumpkin and spinach curry 234

pumpkin with chilli and avocado 94

pumpkin curry 193

pumpkin gnocchi with sage butter 138

pumpkin and hazelnut pesto bites 21

pumpkin and pine nut tagliatelle 149

R

raita 18

ratatouille 98

ravioli

ravioli with herbs 169

ricotta-filled ravioli with fresh tomato sauce 162

spinach ravioli with sun-dried tomato sauce 161

rice

Asian mushroom risotto 142

brown rice and puy lentils with pine nuts and spinach 181

egg fried rice 149

green pilaff with cashews 137

Indonesian coconut and spice rice 146

Jamaican rice with peas 133

khichhari 165

mushroom risotto fritters 185

onion and parmesan pilaff 185

pirozhki 54

pulao 174

saffron rice 165

tomato and cheese risotto cakes 170

vegetable donburi 182

vegetarian dolmades 66

warm lentil and rice salad 70

wild rice, thyme and mixed mushroom pilaff 126

yoghurt rice 166

rice dumplings, steamed 53

ricotta

baked ricotta 65, 194

ricotta and basil with tagliatelle 153

ricotta-filled ravioli with fresh tomato sauce 162

rigatoni with tomato, haloumi and spinach 161

rocket, penne with rocket 141

root vegetables, baked, with sweet ginger glaze 118

S

saffron rice 165

salads

chickpea and olive 81

cooked vegetable 78

curly endive and blue cheese 89

green olive, walnut and pomegranate salad 77

grilled vegetable 82

herbed feta salad 73

Mediterranean lentil 86

orange and date salad 85

snow pea salad 90

spinach and avocado, with warm mustard vinaigrette 85

spinach and nut salad 77

sprout and pear, with sesame dressing 74

tofu salad 89

Tunisian carrot salad 73

warm lentil and rice 70

sesame dressing 74

snow peas

snow pea salad 90

tofu and snow pea stir-fry 217

spaghetti with herbs and tomato 125

spanokopita 206

spiced carrot and feta gnocchi 122

spiced corn 105

spicy chickpea and vegetable casserole 210

spicy eggplant slices 109

spicy eggs and snake beans 237

spicy relish 38

spinach

brown rice and puy lentils with pine nuts and spinach 181

green pilaff with cashews 137

Indonesian pumpkin and spinach curry 234

orange sweet potato and spinach stir-fry 205

pasta and spinach timbales 245

rigatoni with tomato, haloumi and spinach 161

spinach and avocado salad with warm mustard vinaigrette 85

spinach and nut salad 77

spinach pies 30

spinach with raisins and pine nuts 117

spinach ravioli with sun-dried tomato sauce 161

spinach and ricotta cannelloni 242

spinach and ricotta gnocchi 153

spring onion and celery bundles 106

spring rolls 58

sprouts

crunchy stuffed tofu puffs 61

Korean pickled bean sprouts 93

sprout and pear salad with sesame dressing 74

sticky rice pockets, vegetarian 34

stir-fries

almond and broccoli 209

asparagus with sesame seeds 241

orange sweet potato and spinach 205

stir-fries continued
    tempeh stir-fry 217
    tofu, peanut and noodle 125
    tofu and snow pea stir-fry 217
    udon noodle stir-fry 157
sweet garlic eggplant 102
sweet potato
    green curry with sweet potato and
        eggplant 221
    orange sweet potato and spinach
        stir-fry 205
    sweet potato rosti 114
sweet and sour onions 93
sweet and sour tofu 202
sweet vegetable curry 222

T
tagliatelle with asparagus and herbs
    141
tamarind chutney 14
tarragon mayonnaise 21
tempeh stir-fry 217
Thai coconut vegetables 229
tofu
    Asian greens with teriyaki tofu
        dressing 201
    crunchy stuffed tofu puffs 61
    spring rolls 58
    sweet and sour tofu 202
    tofu in black bean sauce 238
    tofu with chilli jam and cashews 214
    tofu, peanut and noodle stir-fry
        125
    tofu salad 89
    tofu and snow pea stir-fry 217
tomato sauce 162
tomatoes
    beans with tomatoes 117
    borlotti bean moussaka 230
    fried green tomatoes 13
    grilled, with bruschetta 33
    linguine with roasted vegetable
        sauce 137
    Mexican tomato bake 213
    okra with coriander and tomato
    sauce 97

    potato and zucchini casserole 249
    ratatouille 98
    spaghetti with herbs and tomato
        125
    tomato and cheese risotto cakes
        170
tortellini with eggplant 129
Tunisian carrot salad 73

U
udon noodle stir-fry 157

V
vegetables
    Asian greens with teriyaki tofu
        dressing 201
    baked root vegetables with sweet
        ginger glaze 118
    Chinese vegetables with ginger 233
    combination vegetable stew 201
    cooked vegetable salad 78
    curried vegetables 62
    grilled vegetable salad 82
    grilled vegetables with garlic
        mayonnaise 22
    individual vegetable pot pies 190
    marinated roasted vegetable dip 26
    noodles with vegetables and herbs
        173
    potato noodles with vegetables
        158
    spicy chickpea and vegetable
        casserole 210
    sweet vegetable curry 222
    Thai coconut vegetables 229
    vegetable coconut curry 237
    vegetable donburi 182
    vegetable korma 205
    vegetable lasagne 198
    vegetable pakoras 18
    winter vegetable casserole
        241

W
wild rice, thyme and mixed mushroom
    pilaff 126

Y
yoghurt rice 166

Z
zucchini
    fettucine with zucchini and crisp-
        fried basil 177
    potato and zucchini casserole 249
    ratatouille 98